A FECKIN' TOUR OF IRELAND

First published 2020 by The O'Brien Press Ltd,
12 Terenure Road East, Rathgar, Do6 HD27, Dublin 6, Ireland.
Tel: +353 1 4923333; Fax: +353 1 4922777
E-mail: books@obrien.ie
Website: www.obrien.ie
The O'Brien Press is a member of Publishing Ireland.

ISBN: 978-1-78849-079-5

1 3 5 7 9 10 8 6 4 2
20 22 24 25 23 21

Layout and design: Brendan O'Reilly
Cover: Brendan O'Reilly
Printed and bound in Drukarnia Skleniarz, Poland.
The paper in this book is produced using pulp from managed forests.

Photo credits

The author and publisher would like to thank the following for permission to use
photographs:

Photos on p.8, p.12, p.22, p.26, p.38, p.44, p.48, p.52, p.64, p.68, p.74, p.78, p.106, p.114,
p.120, p.130, p.132, p.140, p.180, p.184, p.188, p.200, p.204, p.222, p.228, p.234, p.238 and
p.250 courtesy of Shutterstock;
p.16, p.32, p.56, and p.126 courtesy of Colin Murphy;
p.60 David Geib, p.92 Ingo Mehling, p.100 Diliff, p.128 Lisa Harbin,
p.144 Molly Crilly, p. 150 Fiaz Farrelly, p.172 Bob Linsdell, p.176 psyberartist, p.190 Laurel
Lodged, p.192 Sarah Murphy, p.208 spudmurphy, p.214 LoriStrang, p.224 Joebater at
English Wikipedia, p.196 Robert Ashby, p.246 Sarah777,
p.252 Gfox228

Published in:

DUBLIN
UNESCO
City of Literature

A FECKIN' TOUR OF IRELAND

50 Must-do Things

THE GUIDEBOOK THAT'S GINORMOUS CRAIC!

**COLIN MURPHY &
BRENDAN O'REILLY**

THE O'BRIEN PRESS
DUBLIN

Contents

These 50 sites are grouped in their counties, which are
ordered alphabetically.

Fáilte romhat!
(That's 'welcome' to yourself)

So you've arrived in Ireland to see the sights and enjoy the craic. And what better place to start your travels than between the pages of *A Feckin' Tour of Ireland: 50 Must-Do Things?*

Unlike your normal dull-as-ditchwater travel guide, which will fill your head with cold facts and tedious travelogues, *A Feckin' Tour* will enliven your voyage of discovery around the island of Ireland's most famous sights with gansey-loads of Irish wit and blarney – and even enlighten you with more than a few words of deadly Irish slang (see page 255). Full of fascinating facts, amusing anecdotes, hilarious histories and colourful culture, *A Feckin' Tour* is the perfect travelling companion with which to explore Ireland's scenic, historic landscapes and towns, while putting a smile on your face even when the weather's completely wojus!

So 'Céad mile fáilte go hEireann!' For those who don't know, that means 'One hundred thousand welcomes to Ireland!' It's pronounced Kade mee-lah fawl-che guh hair-in. Try saying that when you've had six pints of Guinness and a double Irish whiskey!

This book is dedicated to all those who are involved in helping to maintain Ireland's unique scenic, cultural and historical heritage.

Titanic Belfast at the birthplace of *Titanic*

1. Titanic Belfast

You've seen the movies, you've read the books, you've watched the documentaries, now relive the whole she-bang at the Titanic Belfast visitor attraction.

Now, one has to be honest, there is a question of taste to be considered here, as many people feel that there's something unsettling about a glossy extravaganza with rides and computer-generated wizardry concerning one of the greatest maritime tragedies in history. Still, one could probably make the same argument about the many movies made over the decades. Of course you're on your holliers and you don't want to hear any of that bad taste stuff, so let's bury our collective heads in the sea bed and go full steam ahead towards the iceberg.

All aboard!

First off, the imposing building itself is marvellous, the design based on the hull of the famed ship, though hopefully it's made of sterner stuff.

Within you'll find **nine different galleries** covering various aspects of *Titanic*, from its building to its rediscovery at the bottom of the Atlantic, and all the wet bits in between. The first two galleries give the background to Belfast at the start of the century and its shipbuilding industry, conveniently ignoring the widespread anti-Catholic sectarianism that existed at the time, which was particularly prevalent in Harland & Wolff. Then there's the Launch gallery, which overlooks the ginormous slipway from which *Titanic* was launched. In subsequent galleries you can discover all about the fit-out, and the vast differences between the toffs' and plebs' experience, the initial voyages from Belfast to Southampton to Cherbourg to Cobh in County Cork, during which Irish priest, Fr Francis Browne, photographed many of the unfortunates on board. The Sinking gallery tells the story of the tragedy to the sound of Morse Code and real

survivors recounting their memories and is very touching. Then there's the Aftermath, the Myths & Legends and finally *Titanic* as it is today, with interesting footage from its watery grave.

Overall it's an interesting experience. But this is not a museum as such, and there are no actual *Titanic* artefacts on display. The owners say this is for ethical reasons. Hmmm. Actual artefacts would have real historical and emotional resonances it seems, whereas high-tech gadgetry seems to make it more like a themed ride. But there you go. Make up your own mind. Anyway, it's definitely worth a visit, if only to see the building itself. Oh and by the way, book in advance or you'll end up having to hang around for a couple of hours.

But on the theme of questionable taste, we can get as questionable as the best of 'em! Which is why we'd like to end with this joke:

What do you get if you cross the Atlantic Ocean with *Titanic*? About half way.

INFLATABLE TOY "GUARANTEED UNSINKABLE"

The Dark Hedges, County Antrim

2. The Game of Thrones Tour

The thing is, if you're a fan of the hit HBO show, Northern Ireland is the place to be, as about seventy per cent of the epic fantasy is shot here. Of course if you're not a fan, then terms like Renly Baratheon, Aerys II Targaryen and

Quellon Greyjoy will hold all the attraction for you of being locked into a room with an insurance salesman.

But as the series had hundreds of millions of fans, we'll work on the principle that you have some interest, or at least that your holiday companion is going to drag you along to the locations whether you feckin' like it or not!

The first thing to know is that there are more official tours on offer than there are nudie scenes in the series, which is an awful lot. The tours are mostly by bus, but also by taxi, bike and boat! A lot of them start and end in Belfast, but some also depart from Dublin and Derry (the boat tour starts in Strangford, about 30 km south of Belfast). Any tourist office or hotel lobby in Northern Ireland will have leaflets on myriad options, some of which involve you dressing up in wacky Game of Thrones costumes and waving swords and hatchets like a big eejit.

Among the locations you can visit are:

Magheramore Quarry, 20 km north of Belfast, which, with the help of computer-generated imagery (CGI), doubles as The Wall and the entrance to Castle Black.

Cairncastle, a further 10 km north, was where it all began with the nice beheading of a deserter. The actual castle in the series was also a CGI creation, but you can still walk to the pretty glen along the **Ulster Way** (joining the trail in the Cairncastle car park) and stand beneath the cliffs imagining the deserter's blood squirting from his headless body, or whatever you're into.

To the west you'll see **Slemish Mountain**. Previously famed as the place where St Patrick was enslaved as a youth, the grassy valley beneath it more recently provided the location of a Dothraki camp early in the series.

The beautiful **Cushendun Caves**, further to the north, acted the part of The Stormlands, and where Melisandre gives birth to the shadow assassin. We assume this is all making sense to you?

Follow the northern coast until you reach **Ballintoy Harbour**, otherwise known to GOT experts as Pyke and Iron Islands.

Just down the road is **Larrybane Quarry**, where Brienne bested Ser Loras, just so you know.

Twenty km further west, Downhill Strand is a beautiful beach overlooked by the non-fictional Mussenden Temple, but plays the part of Dragonstone Island and Castle, and is the place frequented by Stannis Baratheon and his often birthday-suited pal Melisandre.

One of the most famous locations of all is The King's Road, or in real life the **Dark Hedges**, which is an eighteenth-century avenue of beech trees. It's about a twenty-minute drive south of Ballintoy Harbour and it was where Arya escaped from King's Landing after her Da had the bad luck to be beheaded.

West of Belfast you'll find **Shane's Castle** on the shores of Lough Neagh, which has had multiple roles as Winterfell, Castle Black, The Land of Always Winter and The

Wildlings Site, and the arched bridge was where Brienne of Tarth and the KingSlayer tried to disembowel each other in a swordfight.

South of Belfast in County Down you'll discover **Castle Ward**, location of Winterfell, the Stark family's gaff in season one. Nearby is **Audley's Castle**, which pretended to be where King Robert Baratheon arrived at Winterfell, was the backdrop of Robb's Camp and where Alton Lannister is imprisoned with Jaime. Still with us?

To the west the ruin of **Inch Abbey** is the location for House Frey's stronghold 'The Twins', protecting the Riverlands, and further west again **Tollymore Forest Park** is known to GOT enthusiasts as the Haunted Forest, and basically every other forest scene was shot here.

So there you go. Hop on the bus, the bike or the car and immerse yourself in an imaginary world of people being gutted with an axe, burned alive by a dragon or having orgies while bathing in pig's blood. All good family entertainment!

After the orgy scene fancy popping down to Ballintoy for fish & chips?

Basalt columns at The Giant's Causeway, County Antrim

3. The Giant's Causeway Coastal Route

This is a crackin' 200-km scenic drive from Belfast to Derry that's packed with sights scenic, historic and alcohol!

Follow the A2 and just north of Belfast you'll come to the pleasant seaside town of **Carrickfergus** and its waterfront castle, which as yet has not featured in *Game of Thrones*, but give it time. It's still in almost perfect nick despite having been built in the twelfth century. Incidentally this route takes in some of the *Game of Thrones* locations previously mentioned, such as Cairncastle, the Cushendun Caves and Ballintoy, so we won't repeat these at the risk of boring you.

Further up the coast between Glenarm and Cushendun you'll encounter the beautiful scenic drive past the nine **Glens of Antrim**. Wander from the coast if you can, and explore the gorgeous glens, and if you're not too lazy, take some of the lovely waymarked walking trails.

From Cushendun follow the Torr Road out to the magnificent **Torr Head**, which affords views

of bonnie Scotland on a clear day. After the town of Bally-castle follow the coast to **Carrick A Rede**, and its famous rope bridge, originally built for fishermen to cross to the tiny, but beautiful island – cross it on a windy day and pretend you're Indiana Jones.

A short drive further west you come to the crème de la crème of the drive – the Giant's Causeway. It's worthy of a lengthier bit...

The Giant's Causeway

At first glance you might think the Giant's Causeway was the work of thousands of sculptors chiselling skilfully away for centuries. You see, it's hard to believe that you're looking at a natural phenomenon. But sure enough, this amazing **UNESCO World Heritage Site** is the result of volcanic activity. It's made up of roughly forty thousand interlocking, hexagonal basalt columns, some twelve metres high, sitting on a jagged promontory that runs from steep cliffs and vanishes beneath the waves. You can even clamber about on the columns, although one wonders how much longer that'll be allowed.

Tall tale

So where does the Giant's Causeway get its name? According to Irish mythology, the giant, Finn MacCool (and no, that's not the name of a McDonald's ice-cream) was always at loggerheads with the Scottish giant Benandonner.

When the Scot challenged him to a duel one fine day, Finn fashioned thousands of hexagonal columns to fit neatly together and built a causeway from Ireland to Scotland so the pair could meet and kick the bejaysus out of each other. But Finn was so tired afterwards that he fell asleep. Before long, Finn's wife heard the thunderous footsteps of Benandonner approaching, so the quick-witted cailín grabbed the baby's bonnet and blanket and put them on her husband. When Benandonner started roaring for Finn to fight him, Finn's wife told him to shush or he'd wake the baby. Benandonner took one look at what he thought was Finn's baby, decided that if his baby was that big then Finn must be the giant of all giants, turned and legged it, destroying the causeway behind him so that Finn couldn't follow. Sounds totally plausible to us.

The geology bit

About sixty million years ago, there was an awful lot of volcanic activity around Antrim and a lava plateau formed, which then cooled and began to contract and fracture, the same way dried mud does. When cooling rates are uniformly distributed, lava fractures evenly, leading to tall, mostly hexagonal columns. But really, isn't the Finn Mac Cool explanation much better craic?

Best foot forward

If you get the weather and you fancy taking in the sights and sounds of the Giant's Causeway on foot, there are a number of walks in the area. You'll find information on walking routes in the Visitor Centre or online, and many of them follow the cliff top, which if you've the time, you really should do, as the views are decidedly splendiferous.

Visitor Centre

This was designed to reflect the natural architecture of the Causeway and it's an interesting building with lots of exhibits within about the geology of the area, and you have to pay a fee to enter, even if you're using only the restaurant or gift shop. The Giant's Causeway itself is free, so you need to pay for a ticket only if you want to get the bus. If you choose to walk, you should pay nada, nil, nought, zip. However, you will have to pay for the car park separately. What a rip-off! But don't let the gobshites deter you. Because although The Giant's Causeway is not enormous, it is beautiful and a truly natural wonder that shouldn't be missed.

Last but not least of our highlights of our coastal drive, and just a short drive to the south of the Causeway is the **Bushmills Distillery**. The Scots claim to have invented whiskey, but let's scotch that once and for all (ha ha). Bushmills is the oldest licensed distillery on the planet, having been granted a licence to distil in 1608 by King James I. So stick that up yer kilt! There are regular, fascinating tours of the old distillery and you'll get to sample a few nips of our famously smooth Irish whiskey. Not to be missed. Just don't drive anywhere afterwards!

Are you aware that drinking Scotch in Ireland is a serious offence?

Loop Head Lighthouse, County Clare

4. Loop Head Peninsula

Here's a perfect opportunity for an enthralling and appropriately looped drive of about 50 km. You could probably do it in a couple of hours — but where's the fun in that? Alternatively you could spend a couple of weeks here, not to mention years, for that matter!

Let's kick off at the pretty seaside town of **Kilkee**, with its gorgeous horseshoe-shaped Blue Flag beach. There are stunning cliff-top walks just to the west of town, long ones for the energetic, short ones for the lazy sod! Charlotte Brontë honeymooned here and the great poet Tennyson was a frequent visitor, so it's obviously an inspiring little hamlet. There's also a statue of **Richard Harris** (unveiled by Russell Crowe in 2006) depicting him playing racquet-ball – the actor won a competition four times in a row in Kilkee, where he spent most of his youthful summer holidays.

Take the R487 and then the R488 to **Carrigaholt**, about 10 km away. This sleepy fishing village sits on the north of the Shannon Estuary, which is a favourite spot for all types

The Whiskey-Bottle-Nosed Dolphin

of bird and sea life. Here's your chance to do a little dolphin-watching – there are daily trips from the pier to view the colony of over two hundred of Flipper's cousins. The village also boasts the ruin of a fifteenth-century castle, and a small beach.

Take the L2002 west, which hugs the coast for a while, but watch for the fork after about 5 km – there's a stone marker telling you you're in Kilclogher – and take the road to the left, which will return you to some great scenic views of the rocky coastline. This will eventually lead you to Kilbåha, a tiny village where you have the opportunity for some refreshments in the local hostelry.

Continue on the R487 out to Loop Head itself, where you'll find a **nineteenth-century lighthouse** that you can visit. There's been a lighthouse of some form here for centuries – it originally, consisted of a coal burning brazier on a platform on the roof of the keeper's home and you can still see part of the old cottage nearby. But really you're here for the scenic views, which may be had aplenty in the short looped walk around the lighthouse.

Drive (or cycle) back along the R487 until you see the

coast road to the left (L2000) and watch for a brown sign for **The Bridges of Ross**. These were a trio of amazing sea arches – until two of the feckers collapsed, yet the plural version of the name persists. But the rugged coastline is still worth a visit even if all three were banjaxed.

CHIROPODIST

'...And reports of severely fallen arches at Bridge of Ross...'

Rejoin the R487 a bit further on, but take a left after about 2 km – basically try to hug the northern coast of the peninsula. The coastal route is a joy, and you'll see a couple of sea stacks, including **Oileán an Fhéaráin**, which is a protected natural heritage island, and **Bishop's Island**, which was joined to the mainland about a thousand years ago and still has the ruins of a church and a beehive hut. Hope the monks weren't stuck out there when the bridge collapsed.

And soon after, you'll be back in Kilkee for a lovely fresh seafood dinner and a couple of pints in one of the town's many welcoming pubs!

Limestone pavement, The Burren, County Clare

5. The Burren

Just a few kilometres to the east of the Cliffs of Moher you'll discover The Burren National Park, which is an amazing moon-like landscape that's jammers with fascinating rock formations, unusual flora and fauna, fossilised sea creatures, prehistoric monuments and people in silly-looking walking gear.

It is way beyond the scope of this small, but wonderful book to do The Burren justice, but there are a squillion other books available to explain every little rock, plant and buzzing insect that you might encounter. Nevertheless, if, like most simple folk, you haven't the time or inclination to study the intricacies of the late Quaternary Period or the Dactylorhiza Marsh Orchid, here's a quick run down on the locality.

Geology, nature and other stuff

The unique area covers about 250 sq km and was formed roughly about the same time as the Cliffs of Moher. It was once under the sea, which explains the presence of fossilised sea urchins, corals and other long dead fishy things.

You won't see any green fields or bogs in The Burren – it is almost devoid of soil and consists mostly of ginormous pavements of limestone called 'clints' with vertical fissures in them called 'grikes'. Beneath your feet is a wonderland of caverns, where most of the bucketing rain ends up. But unless you're an expert pot-holer, these are unfortunately a no-no.

Mullaghmore is an impressive-looking hill one hundred and eighty metres high and consisting of sloping circles of rock piled one on top of the other, and overlooking a group of small loughs to the east and south, making the view on a fine day (in your dreams!) stupendous. Sitting just below it

is the equally impressive **Slieve Rua**, sculpted by nature into winding, rising walls of rock.

Nestling between the countless fissures loads of unusual plants may be observed, including many that would normally be found only in the Mediterranean, the Alps or the Arctic, and botanists still haven't figured out exactly why, the gobshites. Wildflowers abound, particularly in spring and summer, and the green-fingered reader might be happy to discover over twenty types of orchid and ferns, alpine gentians, bloody cranesbills, sheets of mountain avens, yellow hoary rockroses and blue and pink milkwort and a gazillion others. If that read like ancient Swahili to you, don't worry, to enjoy the flora all you have to do is stand, look and breathe in the fresh Burren air.

Lepidopterists will also relish a Burren visit. (No, they're not werewolves, that's lycanthropists, ye big eejit.) As butterfly enthusiasts, they'll appropriately enthuse at the sight of more than thirty different types, colourfully flittering and fluttering from plant to plant.

Burren history rocks!

People have been hanging around the Burren for about 8,000 years, leaving behind lots of their fascinating junk for us to put in museums (Clare Museum in Ennis, for example, has lots of this stuff). Items include stone tools, pottery and weapons, such as axes, which were presumably

used by Stone Age folks to brain each other when fighting over the local cave lads or lasses.

There are many megalithic tombs and monuments, the most impressive being the **Poulnabrone Portal Dolmen**, which has a massive capstone about ten square metres in size, resting, seemingly precariously, on smaller upright stones, that themselves are two metres tall. The capstone weighs roughly ten metric tons, so you can be sure some poor neolithic eejit put his back out lifting that lot.

Although we mentioned earlier that caving was strictly for pot-holers, we sort of lied, as the nice Clare people have developed **Aillwee Cave** into a wonderful attraction. This is definitely worth a visit, and you can experience beautiful caverns, bridged chasms, an impressive underground waterfall, a frozen waterfall, the remains of extinct brown bear bones and of course stalactites and stalagmites.

Another impressive sight in The Burren is **Caherconnell Stone Fort**, only about a kilometre south of the Poulnabrone

Dolmen. It was built around the tenth century, and utilising the gansey-load of rocks lying about the place our medieval ancestors built a wall over forty metres in diameter, three metres thick and three metres high – and you thought putting up that feckin' kitchen shelf was tough.

Take a walk on the wild side

But really folks, if you truly want to appreciate the wonders of The Burren, you have to walk the walk, because what you've read above is a mere glimpse through nature's keyhole. What's more, the area is littered with medieval churches, monasteries, castles, forts and scenery so beautiful it would bring a tear from a glass eye, as they say in County Clare.

And there are walks aplenty to be had, either guided or of the do-it-yourself variety, many of them way-marked. There are short walks for the 'ambulatory-challenged', medium walks for a joyful, educational outing, or more demanding all-day walks that might give you blisters, but will guarantee that you'll enjoy that pint all the more when you reach the pub at the end of the trail!

Ah, lovely!

The Cliffs of Moher on Ireland's Wild Atlantic Way

6. The Cliffs of Moher

First off, if you suffer from acrophobia, or fear of heights, the spectacular Cliffs of Moher are probably not the place for you. Come to think of it, if you suffer from basiphobia, cremnophobia, ornithophobia or thalassophobia (respectively the fear of falling, cliffs, birds, and the ocean), you should probably give them a miss also. On the other hand, if you merely suffer from hippopotomonstrosesquipedaliophobia, or the fear of long words, you'll be perfectly fine. Mind you, while at the cliffs, you'll hear people using words like extraordinarily pulchritudinous and monumentally grandiose to describe them.

The Cliffs of Moher are the most visited natural tourist attraction in Ireland. They soar to two hundred and fourteen metres above the sea at their highest point, dropping to a still impressive only one hundred and twenty metres at the Hag's Head rock to the south. And there are 8 km of path to stroll along the cliff top. Surprisingly though, they are not Ireland's highest sea cliffs. That honour belongs to the Slieve League cliffs in Donegal, which also happen to be the highest in Europe. But what sets Moher apart is their sheerness, which is quite absolute, and gives you the impression you've reached the far end of the feckin' world!

The geology and history bit

The cliffs have been around for quite a while, or as we say in Ireland, yonks. They were formed during the Carboniferous period, which of course you know happened about three hundred and twenty million years ago. You'll find this hard to believe, but at that time the vague lump that would become Ireland was part of a warm, sub-tropical estuary. The area around the cliffs was part of a huge river delta and as silt and sand were washed down, the delta got bunged up and formed a series of low hills, which extended far beyond where the cliffs meet the sea. As the days went by, not to mention the eons, the relentless Atlantic waves battering the bejaysus out of the land caused ginormous rock falls, until, eventually, the land was sculpted into the majestic scene we see today. The cliffs are in a constant state of evolution. Just don't be around when a big bit decides to collapse.

Moving forward 319,998,412 years takes us to 1588, the year of the Spanish Armada. After their defeat by the English Navy in the English Channel, the remaining Spanish ships tried to leg it to safety by sailing towards the North Sea and then around Scotland and south along the west coast of Ireland. This was a bad move as much of Ireland was under control of the English back then. As many as thirty of the eighty or so ships sailed too close to the Irish coast and foundered in heavy seas. At the time, the High Sheriff of County Clare was one Boetius Clancy. He was standing at the top of the Cliffs of Moher when he spotted two Spanish galleons. He reported his sighting and received orders to seize any Spanish who landed and to execute them. Many ships were subsequently wrecked on the Clare coast and Boetius was responsible for hanging hundreds of survivors pronto. As many as five thousand sailors were eventually executed all along the coast of Ireland. However, legend has it that quite a few slipped though the nets, were hidden by the sympathetic Irish peasants and subsequently took a fancy to pretty local cailíns, resulting in lots of olive-skinned babies living along the west of Ireland. Olé to that.

By the start of the nineteenth century, tourism among

the wealthy classes of Europe had taken off and the cliffs were a must-see for these filthy rich dudes. A wealthy local landowner, Cornelius O'Brien, decided to do his bit for the tourist industry, so he built **O'Brien's Tower** near the highest point of the Cliffs, as a viewing area for nineteenth-century visitors, just in case they weren't high enough already. He also built a wall along the cliffs, made from Liscannor flagstone, and what survives of it, now restored within the Visitor Centre grounds, may still be seen.

The nineteenth-century **Moher Tower** is a partial ruin to be found at the southern end of the cliffs. It was built to watch for a possible Napoleonic invasion that never arrived.

OMG! We're being attacked by a swarm of white locusts!

You've the binoculars the wrong way around again, dear.

Birds and wildlife

The cliffs boast an extraordinary diversity of birds, which you can observe swooping and soaring on the rising air currents from your safe perch atop the precipice. It's a good idea to bring along a pair of binoculars to observe some of the ornithological goings-on close-up. The majority of the nesting birds constitute about twenty species, and the cliffs are an **EU Special Protection Area**. There are guillemots, razorbills, puffins, kittiwakes and fulmars, herring gulls, terns, skylarks and, every now and then, a lucky visitor glimpses an endangered peregrine falcon or a chough. Of course if you don't know the difference between a sparrow and a swan, then most of the above will be quite meaningless. Even so, it can be wonderful simply to stand and watch myriad birdlife cutting graceful, majestic arcs above the Atlantic waves, and to listen to the symphony of birdsong.

Non-winged wild creatures are also plentiful in the sea below and on occasion you may even catch a glimpse of a ginormous basking shark, the second-largest fish on the planet after the whale shark. These guys have an enormous mouth, even when compared to Donald Trump's. It is so large you could stand upright inside its jaws, but don't be too worried – you wouldn't taste too good to them as they only eat plankton.

Sometime visitors to the waters below are humpback, blue and fin whales, and there are dolphins, porpoises, otters and seals aplenty. You'll just need an eagle eye to spot them.

The Visitor Centre

A plague struck Ireland in the 1990s – a plague of so-called 'Interpretive Centres', fancy (or sometimes ugly) buildings erected near famous tourist sites to help visitors 'interpret' them. The Cliffs of Moher was no exception, but luckily they got the architecture just right. The building was designed to minimise the impact on the landscape and achieves this splendidly because it is virtually buried in a hillside. Within you'll see an exhibition that brings to life the area's geology and wildlife, audio-visual displays, restaurants, toilets and, of course, gift shops, providing an opportunity to buy your 'Cliffs of Moher' T-shirt. With any luck they'll even be selling our hilarious range of 'Feckin' Books', which are something no self-respecting tourist should leave Ireland without.

Lights, camera, action!

The Cliffs of Moher have enjoyed a starring role in countless movies and television series. And while the quality of the movies has varied greatly, the cliffs deserved an Oscar every time. Here are some of the best known:

Burke & Hare (2010)
Harry Potter & the Half Blood Prince (2009)
Into the West (1992)
Hear My Song (1992)
The Princess Bride (1987)
The Mackintosh Man (1973)
Ryan's Daughter (1970)
The Guns of Navarone (1961)

Blarney Castle, County Cork

7. Blarney Castle

If you were to ask someone in, say, Turkmenistan or Burkina Faso to name a famous tourist destination in Ireland, they'd probably say 'Blarney Castle'. No actually, they'd probably say 'what the hell is Ireland?' But you get our drift.

The legendary Blarney Stone has found fame far and wide for its supposed power to bestow the 'gift of the gab' or elocutionary eloquence, arguably making it the most famous rock in the world. Not bad for a lump of 350 million-year-old bluestone.

Sealed with a kiss

Many people wrongly define 'blarney' as 'insincere talk designed to mislead', or to put it more colloquially 'bullshit'. But that's rubbish! A well-known Irish American archbishop called Fulton J Sheen summed blarney up best when comparing it to 'baloney': 'Baloney is flattery so thick it cannot be true; blarney is flattery so thin we like it.' In other words, those on the receiving end of blarney welcome the experience.

The famed **Blarney Stone** is part of the battlements of **Blarney Castle**, next to the village of (surprise, surprise) **Blarney, which is 10 km from Cork City**. In order to acquire the 'gift of the gab' you have to kiss the Blarney Stone, a process that requires you to ascend 120 steps up an ancient spiral staircase, during which ascent your face will be about three centimetres from the arse of one of the other roughly 500,000 people who annually pucker up, so you can expect to wait some time queuing on the battlements before your turn comes. When the moment arrives, you have to lie on your back with your head projecting out over a twenty-six-metre drop, crane your neck back and plant your slobbering lips on the stone, which is set

BLARNEY

BLATHER

BALONEY

into the battlements, and which has recently had thousands of other slobbering lips kissing it in quick succession.

Legendary

How did the Stone get its magical power? One of the most popular legends involves the fifteenth-century local Lord, Cormac Laidir MacCarthy, who had a looming court case and was worried he'd lose. So he prayed to the Irish Goddess of love, Clíodhna, who told him to kiss the first stone he saw on his way to court, and because Clíodhna was a right stunner (her very name means 'shapely'!) Cormac was putty in her hands. At court he found he could charm the pants off everyone and the case was dismissed. So he had the stone set into the battlements for evermore.

Another tale concerns a descendent of Cormac Laidir, one Cormac Teige MacCarthy, who was commanded to surrender Blarney and its lands to Queen Elizabeth I. An old woman told Cormac to kiss a particular stone in the parapet,

and Cormac then apparently so charmed the besieging Earl of Leicester, that the Queen referred to his accounts of Cormac's eloquent chatter as 'all blarney'. Incidentally, Queen Elizabeth never managed to take the castle. Ha ha.

And there are many more tall tales to explain the Blarney Stone's amazing powers. But if you really want the complete low down, there's this fantastic little book called *A Big Pile of Blarney!*, which sells like hot cakes it's so good, informative and witty. Now, what were the names of the authors again?

The history bit

In 1446, one of Ireland's greatest chieftains, Cormac Laidir (meaning 'the strong') MacCarthy, decided the oul' homestead needed a makeover, demolished the old gaff and built a shiny new castle, which mostly still stands today. Blarney Castle featured machicolations – an opening in the floor around the rim of the battlements, which allowed the inhabitants to chuck big rocks, boiling oil and chamber pot contents down on the heads of their enemies. The Blarney Stone is part of this structure.

The castle withstood many an attack, including the attempt mentioned above by Queen Elizabeth I's armies (and probably her leggies as well). It survived for two hundred years before being finally taken in 1646 by one of that murdering geebag Cromwell's cronies, Lord Broghill. He despised Catholics and would have chopped them into mincemeat had he caught any, but when he got inside he discovered they'd all disappeared via secret underground tunnels.

The castle was returned to the MacCarthy clan in 1661 by Charles II, but just a couple of generations later it was seized in the Williamite Wars and the Brits had it again! It eventually ended up in the hands of the Colthurst family in the nineteenth century, who still occupy the estate to this day.

Among the most famous kissers have been Winston Churchill, Sir Walter Scott, US President William H Taft, Jackie Kennedy, Laurel and Hardy, Michael Jackson, Prince and Mick Jagger, whose lips actually covered the entire area of the Stone.

Out and about

The castle enjoys a very pretty woodland setting in **Blarney Castle Gardens**, which offer the visitor a multitude of paths and tracks and little historical curiosities.

Blarney House is a magnificent baronial-style mansion built in 1874 and set in the middle of the parklands. It features pinnacles, crow-stepped gables and a multitude of conical-capped turrets. It also has a gorgeous interior and views overlooking the small **Blarney Lough**. You can visit it in summer.

Nearby **Blarney village** is one of the last so-called 'estate villages' in Ireland – that is, a village built by the estate landlord for house and farm workers. The picturesque village is dominated by a grassy square where locals and tourists congregate during the summer to sip their lattes and eat their sambos. There is a handful of good pubs, a hotel and shops, and there's a scenic 5-km walk called the **Blarney Way**. This takes in the slightly weird **Round Tower of Waterloo**, which isn't really a round tower and has nothing to do with Waterloo – it was a folly built by a nineteenth-century priest who'd clearly been at the altar wine.

So there you have it, beautiful visitor. It is such a joy to have such an intelligent and attentive reader, and one so good-looking and witty. Your kindness is a balm to all who encounter it and somehow you make time stop and fly at the same time. Honestly, you light up every room you enter like a candle in the darkness and if we could reach from the pages of the book and hug you, we would.

Feckin' Blarney Stone! See what it does to you?

If I hear one more bit of blarney, we're getting divorced.

My God you're lovely when you're angry.

St Finbarr's Oratory, Gougane Barra Forest Park, County Cork

8. Gougane Barra

A huge glacier gouged out a big lump of County Cork during the last Ice Age, resulting, happily, in the magical, tranquil area known as Gougane Barra. This was actually Ireland's first official **National Park** and it's easy to see why. It lies about 70 km west of Cork City or about 20 km northeast of Bantry and it should be a deffo on your 'things to see in Cork' list.

The history bit

The park consists of a glacial lough nestling amid steep-sided hills that are largely forested. There is a small island in the lough linked to the land by a causeway. The landscape was so remote, and the valley so secluded that it inspired the sixth-century monk, St Finbarr, to build a monastery on the island, although little trace of that remains. In the eighteenth century, a local priest called Fr Denis O'Mahony retreated to the island. The remains of the structures he built are well preserved, and may incorporate some of Finbarr's original building. During the penal times (seventeenth/eighteenth century), when the Brits tried to force us holy Catholics to convert to wicked Protestantism

45

by banning masses and hunting down priests, the island became a really important place for Catholics to celebrate mass without the threat of having their heads blown off with a musket. (BTW, there's a fantastic book about that called 'The Priest Hunters', by a relatively unknown but brilliant author...!) In the nineteenth century, a pretty little oratory was built, which has a lovely interior and is a very popular place for weddings, just in case you feel like tying the knot while you're here.

Take a hike!

The surrounding hills are covered in beautiful woodland, with a series of walking paths, some gentle, some ascending the steep slopes but providing wondrous views of the valley to reward you for knackering your weary legs.

There's also a hotel with a restaurant and bar as you enter the valley, along with a gift shop and get this...a **thatched toilet**, which has been voted as among the top one hundred toilets in the world! And in such an amazing landscape, what better place to answer nature's call?

My bucket list? Well, The Pyramids of Egypt, The Great Wall of China, The Thatched Toilet of Gougane Barra...

Cork's English Market has been trading since 1788

9. The English Market, Cork

Always a popular stopping point for visitors to Cork city, but in recent years its become a must, thanks to a visit in 2011 by that most English of all Englishwomen, Queen Elizabeth II. But more of that anon.

The history bit

The market is slap bang in the middle of the city, it actually has no really genuine English connections and the food sold there is almost all proudly artisan Irish. Apparently though there used to be another market nearby called 'The Irish Market' so when the new place of trade was established in 1788, the council gave it the name to distinguish the two, many of the council members being of English extraction. The building was partially destroyed in 1980 by a fire but was lovingly restored to its former glory.

Finger lickin' good

The market has an attractive double-arched entrance on Grand Parade and within you'll find colourful displays of the finest, freshest foods that Cork has to offer, which is a lot, all under a multi-arched wooden ceiling. On the myriad stalls you'll find meat, fish, breads, organic fruit and veg, spices, cheeses and crubeens (pigs' feet, and yes, you read that right!) You'll also find that Cork speciality, tripe and drisheen, which is – are you ready for this? – the edible lining of a cow's stomach served with sliced black pudding made from cow's or sheep's blood, milk, salt and fat, which is then stuffed into the main intestine of a pig which forms the sausage skin. Yummy!

The market also has a selection of clothes and gifts, and there are a number of cafés and restaurants to enjoy a coffee and an Irish scone while listening to the market bustle all about you.

The English Market briefly garnered world attention when Queen Elizabeth visited in 2011, apparently at her own request. There she chatted happily with customers and traders, and none more so than fishmonger Pat O'Connell, who had Her Majesty almost clutching her sides with laughter at his witticisms – enough to earn him an invite to Buckingham Palace. We suspect that he was just fishing for compliments.

We are amused

Looking from the iconic Peace Bridge to Derry City Guild Hall

10. Derry City Tour

There's a whole bunch of tours you can do in Derry, many of the hop-on hop-off variety, others in a cab, and yet others that involve wearing out your shoe leather. They're all great craic and are usually laced with brilliant Northern Ireland humour. And despite much of the city's recent history being a tragic one, you definitely won't be short of entertainment.

The history bit

You might get a teensy-weensy bit confused by the signs you'll see in the city that refer to it as Derry/Londonderry. Let us explain. Up to 1613 the town was called Derry, meaning 'oak grove'. Then in 1613, because of the influence of English businessmen, the town was officially renamed Londonderry. As the centuries passed and conflicts developed between the mostly Catholic Irish nationalists and the Protestant unionists, the name Derry came to be used by the former and the name Londonderry by the latter. Recently, with the Northern Ireland troubles a mostly fading memory, it was agreed to adopt both names so as not to upset either side. But as we want to save on ink, we're going to use the term 'Derry', which actually, most people Proddy or Papist use in everyday conversation anyway.

Whistle stop tour...

Although the tours vary slightly, here's a run down of the sights you're likely to encounter.

The Diamond is a square that is not diamond-shaped, although the low wall surrounding the square's centrepiece sort of is. That centrepiece is the city's memorial to those who died in the two world wars, a thirteen-metre-high pillar atop of which is a winged victory clutching a laurel wreath.

Two hundred metres away is the **Guildhall**, an imposing Victorian building featuring towering stained-glass windows that hopefully cast some colourful light on the boringly dull political goings-on within, it being the seat of the city council.

Derry was the last **walled city** built in Europe and, despite the best efforts of gobshite developers, the walls are still completely intact! They are almost 2 km long and enclose centuries of history.

The Museum of Free Derry brings much of the city's recent history to life, with full multi-media exhibitions on the civil rights movement of the 1960s and '70s, including the Battle of the Bogside, internment and the tragedy of Bloody Sunday.

The Bogside Murals have become an icon of the Troubles, painted mostly on the gable ends of homes and depicting various events from the conflict from a nationalist perspective. One of the most famous gable ends proclaims 'You are now entering free Derry' – and it is just a gable that has been preserved although the actual house has been demolished!

Across the river in the mostly Protestant area, the **Nelson Drive Murals** similarly adorn gable ends, mostly, but depict events from a unionist perspective. You can't have one without the other!

The River Foyle divides the city, sadly not just geographically but, particularly in the past, politically as well. One of the initiatives to put that behind us is the **Peace Bridge**, an elegant cycle and footbridge linking the two sides of town. There is also a pleasant walking path running for several kilometres along the west bank of the river.

Ebrington Square on the east side of the Foyle was previously a military parade ground and barracks, but it is in the process of transforming itself into an artsy, creative place, that often features free public entertainment or major concerts, and there are a couple of good restaurants if you're peckish.

Lough Veagh and Glenveagh National Park

11. Glenveagh National Park

This stunning **National Park** encompasses 170 sq km of sheer natural beauty, a magnificent castle, beautiful gardens and enough walking trails to totally banjax your poor feet.

The history bit

It's not that we want you to feel guilty when you're wandering around Glenveagh enjoying the truly stupendous scenery, gardens and castle. But the thing is, the original owner of the land, John Adair, decided back in 1861, that the pesky forty-seven families of scruffy, smelly tenants, were rather spoiling the views, so he promptly evicted the lot and threw them to the mercies of nature. Total scumbag. Still, that was donkey's years ago, and time has provided enough of a buffer to allow us to enjoy the place with a clear conscience. And besides, a later, more enlightened owner, Henry McIlhenny, bequeathed the land and castle to the state in 1983.

Ever get the feeling you're being stalked?

Glenveagh Castle isn't really a castle, to be honest, although it looks like one, with its defensive castellated battlements and its towering keep. Adair had it built in the 1870s as a luxury highland, hunting retreat, and it's not like he was expecting an attack by rampaging tribes of spear-carrying, axe-wielding locals. Having said that, considering the evictions he carried out, maybe he was worried that his ex-tenants might storm the place and give him a good arse-kicking. The castle's setting is majestic, nestled amid trees on the shores of Lough Veagh. There's even a swimming pool – heated at one time! – built into the lakeside. Behind the castle you'll find the beautifully maintained gardens, which are worth a wander for some more photo ops with exotic plants, even if it's raining.

It's only natural

Beyond the castle grounds you'll discover the true attractions of Glenveagh — nature itself, and gansey-loads of walking trails of varying lengths and difficulties through stunning scenery. You might even be lucky enough to glimpse one or two of Ireland's largest herd of beautiful red deer, or even a golden eagle, which was reintroduced a couple of decades ago. All in all, as they say in Donegal, Glenveagh is only savage!

I'm looking for the swimming pool.

Slieve League cliffs, County Donegal

12. Slieve League

The name in Irish translates as 'grey mountain', but whoever came up with that one must have been feckin' colour blind, as this amazing place is anything but grey. The opposite is actually the case and you'll leave here your head abuzz with an inspiring spectacle of land and sea filled with colour, scents and sounds.

The height of spectacle

Slieve League is actually a mountain, but what makes it unique is that some time in the eons long gone, about half of the yoke was washed away into the sea, resulting in what are said to be the highest sea cliffs in Europe, although that title is disputed by Croaghaun Mountain in Mayo and some

Just my luck.

place in the Faroe Islands that doesn't have brilliant pubs nearby, so that doesn't count.

At six hundred and one metres high, the cliffs are almost three times as high as the more famous Cliffs of Moher, though they're not as sheer. But every cloud has a silver lining, and because of the slight slope, vegetation can cling to the rock face in parts, turning it into a tapestry of moss, grass, wildflowers and rock upon which thousands of birds have made their home.

There's a large car park about a kilometre from the viewing area, or if you're feeling lazy, you can open the gate and drive up to **Bunglass Viewing Point**, although this car park is small and can become jammers very quickly, especially in summer, in which case you'll have to drive back down and walk up anyway. Serves you right! Lazy sod.

What can one say about the views? Dazzling? Ravishing? Spectacular? Heavenly? Even the thesaurus fails us! But don't stop at the viewing point. Bring your walking shoes and brave the famous **'One Man's Path'** (aka 'One Man's Pass') that ascends to the summit, so called because in parts only one man, or woman, can traverse it. You don't have to be a mountaineer to climb it, you just have to be not a complete

eejit and take any chances. The views from the path of
Donegal Bay, the distant Sligo Mountains and the ocean
below are, needless to say (back to the thesaurus), sensa-
tional, out of this world, phenomenal...

St Patrick's Day Parade, O'Connell Street, Dublin

13. The St Patrick's Day Parade

Back about fifteen years, the St Paddy's Day Parade in Dublin (as we call it in Ireland) had deteriorated into a boring mix of dreary brass bands and floats that were essentially giant ads for everything from booze to chocolate bars to cars. Luckily someone finally shouted 'Hold your feckin' horses!' to this pile of baloney. Since then, the parade has been transformed into a wonderfully creative celebration of all things Irish and of Ireland's connections with peoples all over the globe. The parade happens on 17 March, St Patrick's Day (surprise, surprise), but in Dublin our celebration of our patron saint has now expanded to become the St Patrick's Day Festival which usually lasts about four or five days and will always encompass a weekend, which is great if the seventeenth has the bad manners to fall midweek.

Parades are held in gansey-loads of towns big and small, but our focus here is on the main event in Dublin. It kicks off at noon, but if you're planning to attend, grab your spot along the route as early as possible, as every path, lamppost, railing etc will be jammers with people five deep by the time the first airs from the Swaziland Juggling Brass Band and Acrobatic Troupe march by. It starts at **Parnell Square**

Deadly!

on the north of the River Liffey, proceeds down O'Connell Street, twists around past **Trinity College** into **Dame Street** past **Dublin Castle** and **Christ Church Cathedral** and then turns appropriately into Patrick Street beneath **St Patrick's Cathedral** before the marchers can rest their banjaxed limbs in Kevin Street. It is a wildly colourful affair, featuring all sorts of ginormous mythical, literary or historical creations, swirling dance troupes in myriad bright colours, bands and dancing girls from all over the world, guys dressed as St Patrick, others dressed as Dracula or Gulliver riding unicycles, jugglers tossing chainsaws in the air, or sometimes a combination of all of the above! The annual attendance in Dublin is about half a million people, about half of whom will be wearing gigantic leprechaun hats, and the parade lasts about two hours. Incidentally, traditionally you're supposed to pin fresh shamrock somewhere about your person on St Patrick's Day.

After the parade the centre of Dublin can become a teeny weeny bit chaotic – it's only two o'clock and there's a lot of pub time left. But generally the mood is good-natured and often there is a big police (Garda) presence, and they usually join in the craic as well. As night descends, many of Dublin's buildings turn green, not to mention some of the eejits who've been getting rat-arsed all day.

The broader festival involves a whole series of events such as exhibitions, tours, live music for all tastes, children's events, live theatre, food stalls etc., and the whole shebang culminates with a fireworks display over the Liffey. It's a great time to be Irish – and even if you're not Irish, you'll be awarded temporary Irish nationality, the only requirement being that you have great craic!

67

The Baily Lighthouse, Howth, County Dublin

14. The Dublin Coastline

During the 1980s, Ireland got two new acronyms: DIRT and DART. DIRT stood for Deposit Interest Retention Tax (yuck!) and DART stood for Dublin Area Rapid Transit (yippee!) Thanks to the DART you can explore the entire Dublin coastline with ease. There are three city centre DART stations, Pearse, Tara Street and Connolly. So let's make tracks.

Heading south

On your journey, you'll pass lots of interesting yokes like the **Grand Canal Dock**, the **Aviva Stadium** and the popular **Sandymount Strand**, but let's make your first stop at **Blackrock** village. The DART will leave you only one minute's walk from the main street, which is cute enough, and has plenty of pubs, restaurants, art galleries and hanging flower baskets. If, instead of heading into the

Watch out - they swoop down and steal your sushi.

69

village, you turn right when you exit the station, you'll find a narrow lane back along the rail line, which, after 100 m, will lead you into **Blackrock Park**. This is a pretty park with sea views, a pond, a Victorian bandstand and a **Martello Tower**, which were built by the Brits to watch for a Napoleonic invasion that never came.

Back on the train we're heading for **Dún Laoghaire** (pronounced *doon leer-eh*), one of Ireland's principal ferry ports, and its two piers alone are worth a visit, especially the east pier. Each one stretches 1.3 km, and the east pier is extremely popular with locals and tourists. You might like to indulge in a stroll to the end, breathing in the sea air, gazing at the bobbing yachts, resenting the rich bastards that own them. Dún Laoghaire itself has lots of well-kept pastel-coloured Victorian residences. The main street, George's Street, has plenty of decent pubs, cafés and restaurants.

Almost next door to Dún Laoghaire is **Sandycove**, which isn't a village really, but is famous for two things – James Joyce and swimming, sometimes in the nip. If you keep following the coast until you come to a rocky promontory, you'll see a nearby Martello Tower and a swimming area known as The Forty Foot. James Joyce resided in the Tower and decided to set the opening scenes of his masterpiece *Ulysses* there. The place is now **The James Joyce Tower and Museum**.

The other place of interest is a bathing area called The Forty Foot, which takes its name not from the depth, but

Can't see Napoleonic invaders, but can see folk swimming in the nip.

from the British 40th Regiment of Foot that used to be stationed here. Men have been swimming here for a few centuries, largely arse-naked, so it was off-limits to women. But after protests, the gents finally relented, and the nudie swimming is now limited to a small area around the corner.

Next stop **Dalkey**, which is the place that Bono took Michelle Obama and the girls out to lunch when she visited in 2013. It's a very pretty and posh seaside village, and its residents have numbered the aforementioned Bono, his buddy The Edge, Van Morrison, Lisa Stansfield, writers George Bernard Shaw and Maeve Binchy, movie director Neil Jordan, Formula One drivers Damon Hill and Eddie Jordan and loads of other very rich head-the-balls.

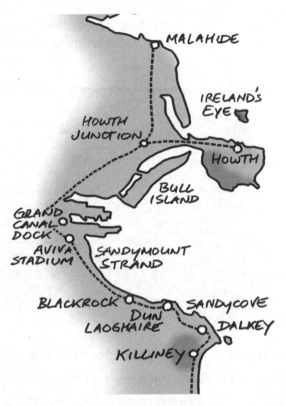

The train ride as you approach **Killiney** is quite beautiful – make sure you sit on the seaward side. Killiney is possibly the most la-di-da suburb in Ireland. People don't light their cigars here with ten-euro notes – they use a ten-euro note to light a fifty-euro note before lighting their cigars with that. Having said that, the village isn't really up to much. Basically a pub and a shop. But go for a relaxing stroll on **Killiney Strand**, or a more energetic one up **Killiney Hill** via its woodland tracks to take in the fab views of Dublin Bay and the Wicklow Mountains.

Heading north

The northwards DART doesn't hug the coastline but the villages of **Howth** and **Malahide** are absolutely worth a trip. Be aware that the DART line splits at Howth junction, the other line going to Malahide. The very attractive Howth was originally a small fishing village and now it's a large fishing village. It has a couple of pretty piers and you'll get the unmistakable whiff of fresh fish, along with the unmistakable whiff of money, as Howth Hill is another of those swanky Dublin neighbourhoods with famous rich folk like U2's Larry Mullen, novelist John Banville and actress Saoirse Ronan. And if you like fresh seafood, you've come to the right place. You can also take a boat trip to the island of **Ireland's Eye** or you can indulge in a spectacular cliff walk, if you have any energy left. All in all, Howth has it all.

Your other choice on the northside is Malahide, a very attractive village with lots of well-kept buildings, tree-lined streets, flowers everywhere in spring and summer and of course nice pubs and restaurants. There's a marina, a two-kilometre beach, Europe's largest model railway and a market every Saturday afternoon, in case you're running short of junk you don't need. And of course there's twelfth-century **Malahide Castle**, set amid beautiful parkland, where you can imagine knights scaling the towers to rescue damsels in distress.

Entrance to Guinness Storehouse, St James's Gate Brewery, Dublin

15. The Guinness Storehouse

Now, there are two ways to approach the Storehouse, and we're not talking about map directions. One is to go there with your cynical hat on. The other is to convince yourself that you are off to experience some genuine history and cultural insight. You'll probably end up with a bit of both.

Ads infinitum

There is no denying that the Guinness Storehouse is possibly the world's largest, self-contained marketing extravaganza. By the time you've reached the seventh floor, your poor eyes will have been exposed to roughly the same number of Guinness logos as there are stars in a galactic supercluster. In fact, when you enter the place, you step into the bottom of the world's largest glass – were it filled with Guinness, it would contain 14 million pints – almost enough to satisfy a hen party from Blackpool. And in case you doubted that you were being exposed to a frenzy of marketing, there is even an 'Advertising Gallery', where you can experience what it was like in the old days to be brainwashed into buying alcohol. Those Guinness marketing boys are some cute hoors, as we

Gee, thanks Mom.

say. Oh, make sure before you leave that you pop into the Guinness Store for some pricey memorabilia. Yes! You are now going to buy a T-shirt, mirror, jug, snooker cue, slippers, tie, golf ball, underpants or knickers, so that you can carry the Guinness message to the world. And besides, isn't it handy to have a reminder when you're putting on your knickers that you should go for a Guinness at your earliest convenience?

History in the making

Ok, ok, enough cynicism. Even if you found that all a bit hard to swallow, at least you won't the Guinness. So, ignoring all of the above, this place is a mecca for beer connoisseurs. The brewery also occupies a fundamental place in the development of Dublin City and is a source of pride for

Hey, think I'm getting that 360° view of Dublin.

Irish people. On your visit, you'll learn that this was once the largest brewery on the planet and still produces two and a half million pints a day. You'll get to see a copy of the lease Arthur Guinness signed for the lands, which was for nine thousand years, thus demonstrating supreme confidence in the longevity of his product. And you'll get to learn about age-old brewing traditions, the craft of coopering, where the water comes from, and the barges on the Liffey, and by the time you've heard all that, which, admittedly, is very interesting, you'll be gagging for a pint of the stuff.

When you've reached the Perfect Pint Bar, a Guinness 'Ambassador' will teach you how not to make a bollox of pulling a pint, which you can then quaff and get your certificate, which you can frame and stick over your mantelpiece alongside the one for nude break dancing you got when you were nineteen.

Last but not least is the Gravity Bar, towering over the brewery, which has a 360-degree view of Dublin, and you get to enjoy a pint (included in your ticket). Anyway, it will probably be the high point of your visit (ha ha).

Fusilier's Arch, Stephen's Green, Dublin

16. Dublin's Heart: Grafton Street, St Stephen's Green, Georgian Dublin, The National Gallery

Grafton Street

Once ranked fifth priciest street in the world, Grafton Street has, happily, fallen out of the line-up of world's most expensive streets in recent years, and there is more to it than posh gobshites flashing branded shopping bags so that you know what rich bowsies they are. There are of course a bunch of international retail chains, but at least some fine Dublin institutions have survived the ravages of globalisation.

Grafton Street was named after Henry Fitzroy, the first Duke of Grafton. Henry was the product of a night of passion between King Charles II and his mistress Barbara Villiers, so Grafton Street is named after a genuine bastard. As an adult, Henry was sent by the British army to assist in the Siege of Cork in 1690, where a well-aimed Irish bullet put a large hole in him. His father, the King, was developing a tract of land in Dublin at the time and Grafton Street was soon transformed into a fashionable residential street and named in honour of Henry.

Starting at the Trinity College end, this is the only section of the street that is not pedestrianised. The nice building behind the wall and railings on your left is the Trinity College Provost's House, but you can't visit that unless you somehow become provost of Trinity. Taking a quick diversion down Suffolk Street, on the left-hand side, in front of a former church, is the most photographed sculpture in Dublin, that of **Molly Malone**. Molly is a generously proportioned cailín famed through the folk song 'Molly Malone' (aka 'Cockles and Mussels'), which has become a Dublin anthem. The statue was erected in 1988 to celebrate Dublin's Millennium and in a flash was christened 'The Tart with the Cart' by Dublin wits.

Having taken a photo with your head next to Molly's boobs, return to the Nassau Street/Suffolk Street junction, turn right, and you're onto the pedestrianised part of Grafton Street. Up ahead is the usual plethora of international fashion and mobile phone stores, junk-food outlets, jewellers, hair salons etc that you will find ad nauseam around the world. Luckily, there are also a couple of uniquely Irish institutions. One such is **Brown Thomas** on your right, which has been around since 1848, catering for the poshest of us Dubs. If you can afford it, this is the place to shop in Dublin, if you want to make a statement that you're feckin' loaded. But if you're not, go in anyway and gape at the suits and dresses that cost the same as your car.

A bit further on the left is **Duke Street**, which has three venerated pubs with literary/Joycean connections, namely

The Bailey, **The Duke** and **Davy Byrne's**, all of which seem to have been there longer than the pyramids. Back to Grafton Street and further along on the right is one of Dublin's most popular and historic landmarks: **Bewley's Oriental Café**, which has just undergone a major refurbishment. Don't let the 'oriental' confuse you – no Egg Foo Yung in here. What you will get is a glorious cup of coffee or tea, a lovely pastry, breakfast, lunch or dinner in a wonderful ambience of chatter amid dark-stained wood and glass. And watch for the beautiful **stained-glass** windows that were created in 1931 by arguably Ireland's greatest stained-glass artist, Harry Clarke. Just try not to put your elbow through one accidentally.

Further up, turn right into **Harry Street** and **Bruxelles** pub, a popular spot for generations of Dubs, and where the band Thin Lizzy played their early gigs. Outside is a life-sized statue of the band's leader, **Phil Lynott**, who is one of Ireland's rock music legends. Thin Lizzy achieved international acclaim with hits such as 'Whiskey in the Jar' and 'The Boys are Back in Town'.

St Stephen's Green

At the top of Grafton Street is St Stephen's Green — you can't miss it — it's the big green thing with all the trees. The park covers a lovely 22 acres and the noise of the traffic seems to vanish as soon as you enter — the circumference was planted with a wall of shrubs to achieve just that effect. Once inside, you can wander the flower-lined paths that snake around the pond, view the statues and sculptures, the trees and shrubbery, the bandstands and fountains. That's all you really need to know about the place. Relax. Chill. Look at the flowers. Listen to the gently sprinkling fountain.

But just in case you want some history, we're here to please. Let's start with the leper colony that used to be here. But relax, that was in the seventeenth century. The place back then was a big swamp and the City Assembly decided that the area should be 'wholie kept for the use of the citizens to walke and take open aire', although mostly this was the preserve of the well-to-do. After that, it became popular as a place for executions and floggings. Crowds would gather to observe some unfortunate gurrier being whipped, strangled, burnt, pilloried, stoned or hanged, though not all at the same time. In 1877 Lord Ardilaun, the wealthy great-grandson of Arthur Guinness, the brewery's founder, decided to buy the land, landscape it and give it to the city. St Stephen's Green was officially opened on 27 July 1880 and, as it was put in a popular song from the early twentieth century:

Dublin can be heaven, with coffee at eleven
And a stroll on Stephen's Green
There's no need to hurry
There's no need to worry
You're a king and the lady's a queen ...

During the 1916 Easter Rising, the rebels used the Green as one of their bases of operation. And evidence of the gun battle can be seen in the main Grafton Street/Fusiliers' Arch entrance, where bullet holes are still visible. An amusing aside to this event gives us an insight into the curious attitudes of the day, as both sides agreed to a brief ceasefire so the park groundsman could feed the ducks.

I notice they didn't have a ceasefire to feed the pigeons.

The centre of the park was originally adorned with a towering equestrian statue of King George II, but poor old Georgie suffered the fate of many other ex-colonial statues when the IRA blew him up in 1937.

Among the things to watch out for are the interesting **Blind Garden** and the artistic installation by the world-renowned sculptor Henry Moore in honour of **WB Yeats**. You'll recognise it when you see a tall piece of metal that looks like it was retrieved from a train-wreck. You'll also find numerous sculptures recalling famous (or infamous) Irish people or events, such as the memorial to the one million victims of the **Great Famine**, or the monument to one of the founding fathers of Irish republicanism, **Wolfe Tone**.

Around the Green, next to Grafton Street, you'll see the **St Stephen's Green Shopping Centre**, designed to look like a conservatory, and music fans may like to note that it was built on the site of the Dandelion Market, where U2 performed their first gig to an audience of fifty people in the dim and distant 1970s.

Walk along the north side of the Green to number fifteen and the charming **Little Museum of Dublin**, located in a beautiful Georgian building and featuring twentieth century memorabilia. Here you'll see stuff like posters of U2's early gigs, product packaging from the 1900s, a first edition of James Joyce's *Ulysses* and loads of interesting bits like that! It's worth taking the guided tour.

Further along, you'll see what is possibly Ireland's most famous hotel, **The Shelbourne**. Despite the owners remaining loyal to the Crown during the Rising, when British soldiers occupied the building, the nationalist porter regularly sneaked on to the roof to signal the British troop movements to the rebels. In 1922, the Irish Constitution was drafted in room 112. Among The Shelbourne's guests down the years have been Stan Laurel, Oliver Hardy, James Cagney, John Wayne, Maureen O'Hara, Elizabeth Taylor, Richard Burton, Orson Welles, Rita Hayworth, John F Kennedy and Jackie Kennedy Onassis. The famous Horseshoe Bar even merited a mention in James Joyce's *Ulysses*. Oh, and Hitler's half brother, Alois Hitler, worked as a waiter there!

Georgian Dublin

Time to get street smart and explore some of Dublin's famed **Georgian architecture**....and to work up a thirst for later. The buildings used to be the townhouses of eighteenth-century toffs but were also home to loads of famous people. Many of the streetscapes are virtually untouched by the march of 'progress'. So let's take a stroll back to the days of cobbled streets, fine gentlemen with top hats and elegant ladies with hooped dresses.

Merrion Square is one of the best-preserved in Dublin, so let's stroll around there, starting at the north-west corner, where you'll see a building called the American College. This is **No. 1 Merrion Square** and was the house where Oscar Wilde grew up. The first two floors have been beautifully restored to the way they would have appeared in Oscar's day, but unfortunately you can only visit as part of a group tour. But for now, let's meet the great Oscar himself, or at least a quirky version of him, which sits inside the park facing his old gaff.

The **Oscar Wilde sculpture** is unusual, to say the least. It shows Oscar reclining on a granite boulder, which

"I don't want to go to heaven. None of my friends are there."

helps explain the sculpture's tongue-in-cheek rhyming nickname – 'The Fag on the Crag'. His seemingly uncomfortable position no doubt accounts for his expression – half grimace, half smile. His colourful clothes are made of precious stones including jade and pink thulite. Nearby the pregnant mot in the nip and the male torso represent Oscar's ambiguous sexual preferences, so make of that what you will.

Walk around the square in a clockwise direction. The doorways of these buildings have become something of an icon of Dublin – some are brightly painted, with the curved fanlight above and often with floral arrangements around them. Also keep an eye out for the circular metal plates you might spot in the ground. These were the 'coal holes' – where the coal was delivered to the house so that the wealthy bowsies upstairs wouldn't have to get their hands dirty. Carry on until you come to the corner of the park. The big building on the left is the **National Maternity Hospital**, which could come in handy if your waters just broke. Turn right. The building at No. 39 used to house the British Embassy, that was until the Bloody Sunday massacre in Northern Ireland in 1972 sparked huge protests and a mob shamefully burned the embassy to the ground. But on to lighter matters.

When you reach the next corner you'll have the opportunity to actually experience what it was like to live in one of these beautiful residences back in the days. Watch for **The**

Georgian House Museum, which is one of the best little museums in Dublin. Inside you'll get a real sense of the 'upstairs-downstairs' lives of the people who lived here, i.e. where they and their servants ate, drank, entertained, dossed around, slept, copulated, dressed and picked their noses. It is complete with all the furnishings and decorations of the time and still features the original interiors.

Continue along Merrion Square South. At No. 58 you'll see the house where 'The Liberator', **Daniel O'Connell**, lived. Dan didn't liberate us from Britain, but from the religious persecution of the Penal Laws.

No. 65 was once the home of **Erwin Schrödinger**, Nobel Prize-winning founder of Wave Mechanics. This is where he came up with the famous Schrödinger Equation. You'll need to learn this off so you can discuss it in the pub later:

$$i\hbar\frac{\partial\Psi}{\partial t} = -\frac{\hbar^2}{2m}\left(\frac{\partial^2\Psi}{\partial x^2} + \frac{\partial^2\Psi}{\partial y^2} + \frac{\partial^2\Psi}{\partial z^2}\right) + V\Psi(x,y,z,t)$$

Got that? Great. Moving along, No. 70 was once the home of **Sheridan Le Fanu**, who, in case you didn't know, was the leading ghost story writer of the Victorian era.

You'll find the former gaff of our legendary, Nobel Prize-winning poet, **WB Yeats** at No. 82. A couple of doors down at No. 84 was once the workplace of renowned Irish

nationalist writer and painter **George William Russell**. Old Russ believed himself to be clairvoyant, so he could read your thoughts. You filthy thing. Wait until you get back to the hotel!

Turn right again and facing the park is a green space and beyond it the back of **Leinster House**, the seat of Ireland's Parliament. Well, actually, this is the original front of the building with its nice lawns and monuments. But not knowing the front from the back sits very well with Irish politicians, who never know whether they're coming or going.

And immediately to the right of that stands the National Gallery...

The National Gallery

Newly reopened in 2017 after a six-year refurbishment, the interior of the original building has frequently been described as 'stunning', or as we say in Dublin, bleedin' deadly. Apparently the renovation unearthed large spaces that no one knew existed, along with magnificent windows that had been walled-off. It's all very impressive indeed, and that's before you even look at the paintings!

The gallery was founded in 1864 and has enjoyed a number of substantial bequests, such as a third of the royalties from the estate of George Bernard Shaw, which has

It's a Bacon.

allowed it to develop a collection of works by some of the art world's really big shot names. Within its various wings you'll find works by **Vermeer**, **Velázquez**, **Picasso**, **Turner**, **Titian**, **Rembrandt** and **Monet** (although they might not all be on display at any one time). And there's a great story behind one of the gallery's most famed possessions. In 1990, the gallery's senior conservator, Sergio Benedetti, was asked to have a look at some paintings in the Jesuits' House of Studies in Dublin, and in the dining room, where it had been for about sixty years, he recognised a priceless, considered-lost **Caravaggio** called **The Taking of Christ**. It's a bit like finding the winning lotto ticket in your waste-paper basket.

And how much will it cost you to visit this treasure house of great art? Absolutely zilch!

Christ Church Cathedral, Dublin

17. Christ Church and St Patrick's Cathedrals

Here's the chance for a bit of spiritual sustenance before you begin drinking religiously. The two venerated churches are very conveniently located just a few hundred metres apart, which was very considerate of those medieval builders for leg-weary tourists. God works in mysterious ways.

Christ Church Cathedral

The original church dates from 1028, when Sitric, the Viking king of Dublin, built the first, wooden Christ Church, after a visit to Rome, which was evidently inspirational. One of Ireland's most renowned saints, **St Laurence O'Toole**, laid the foundation stone to replace the wooden structure in the twelfth century. After he died in Normandy, his heart was preserved in a heart-shaped wooden box and returned to the church where it could be viewed until March 2012, when it was stolen, suspicion falling on rare artefact thieves. It puts a new twist on stealing someone's heart away.

King Henry II of England, who famously ordered the murder of **Archbishop Thomas Becket** in Canterbury Cathedral, attended the Christmas service in Christ Church in 1171 – the first time he received communion after the murder, which made everything all right then.

Later in the century, **Strongbow**, one of the leaders of the Norman invasion of Ireland, would help to fund the completion of the Cathedral, for which he was rewarded with a tomb there. The tomb was destroyed when the roof collapsed in the sixteenth century, and his remains were relocated, and the new tomb is said to contain some of his organs, although which ones doesn't bear thinking about. There is a strange half figure adjoining the tomb, and legend goes that it is his son, who he cut in half after he failed to show courage in battle. But the legend is probably a half-truth (ha ha).

Unfortunately, the head-the-balls who'd designed the original church had decided to put the foundations in a peat bog – oops. Surprise, surprise, almost the entire thing collapsed in 1562. Only the north wall of the original structure survived and it visibly leans – don't jump up and down if you're standing under it. The building stayed much like that for a few hundred years until it was completely rebuilt in the nineteenth century. The church across the road was demolished and the **Synod House** erected there, and the two were joined by an iconic arched walkway. As a result of all the demolition and rebuilding nobody knows which are the original bits and which are the new bits, so Michael Jackson would probably have felt at home there.

After a look at the magnificent stonework and the tomb of Strongbow, head for the **twelfth-century crypt**, which is the oldest surviving structure in Dublin. At sixty-three metres, it is the longest crypt in Ireland or Britain. There is a tale told, and with some substance, of an unfortunate Lieutenant Blacker who was attending a funeral back in 1822 when he wandered away from the mourners in the dimly lit crypt, possibly to have a pee, entered a large underground passage and couldn't find his way out. The passage door was subsequently locked and not opened again for months. To the horror of those opening the door, they found a skeleton picked clean by rats and his sword still clutched in his hand. Around his remains were the skeletons of countless sewer rats, which the officer had felled before they'd finally swarmed over him, eating him alive. Yeuch.

The crypt also displays **stocks** built in 1670 that used to reside outside in Christ Church Place.

One of the most popular curiosities is the mummified cat and rat – nicknamed **Tom and Jerry**. It seems the cat chased the rat into an organ pipe sometime in the mid-nineteenth century and got stuck there, until repair work on the organ revealed their mummified bodies. The cat's pursuit of the rodent is now immortalised in a glass case.

For a small extra fee you can take a guided tour up the eighty or so steps of a winding staircase to the **Belfry Tower**, and visitors can even have a shot at ringing the bells. These bells traditionally ring in the New Year to hordes of absolutely gee-eyed Dubs staggering about on the street outside.

St Patrick's Cathedral

Legend has it that St Patrick began baptising us pagan Irish at a well located beside the site. Because of this, a thirteenth-century archbishop, John Comyn, decided to honour Paddy with a cathedral, and a successor of his, Archbishop Luke, was mostly responsible for the construction. The building's spire, the highest in Ireland at forty-three metres, has literally had its ups and downs. In 1316 the original one blew down in a storm, was replaced in 1370 and collapsed again in 1394. The third version of the spire is still towering over us today. The spire's clock dates from 1560 and was one of the first public clocks in Ireland. Luckily, nobody could read a clock at the time so you always had an excuse not to go home from the pub.

During the Reformation years, St Pat's was batted back

and forth from being a Catholic church to Protestant and back again. During Oliver Cromwell's reign of terror in Ireland, the place fell into disrepair and the gouger held courts martial there, and even supposedly stabled his horses inside. In 1690, the Catholic **King James II** held a Catholic mass there in advance of the Battle of the Boyne. Unfortunately for him, God was out to lunch as he had his arse kicked by William of Orange. Another interesting tomb, and a deliciously gruesome memorial, is that of **Lord Lisburne**, who was killed at the Siege of Limerick. A cannonball struck him – use your imagination to complete the scene. The various bits of Lisburne were interred in the cathedral, with the actual cannonball dangling above him as an eternal reminder.

By the nineteenth century, the Cathedral was pretty banjaxed. Meantime, the people of Ireland had made **Benjamin Lee Guinness** Ireland's richest man by enthusiastically quaffing as much of his product as they could. So Ben decided to give something back by way of restoring the Cathedral. It took five years and about ninety million in today's earnings. Not surprisingly, he is honoured with a statue in the grounds.

Besides having loads of interesting bits 'n' bobs to see, what sets St Pat's apart is that one of its deans happened to be **Jonathan Swift**, writer of, among other things, *Gulliver's Travels*. Many people think he was English, but he was a Dub. He's ours, so hands off!

Swift was dean of St Patrick's from 1713 until he died in 1745. Apparently he used to keep fit by running up the spire stairs. Fair play to him. He also had a famous relation-

Jonathan Swift

ship with Esther John-son, who was the love of his life and who he nicknamed **'Stella'** – her tomb is alongside his in the cathedral.

When not snogging Stella, Swift took time out to write *Gulliver's Travels*, often described as the greatest work of satire in the English lan-guage. It has been made into about three million movies. But Swift was also a tireless worker for the poor, and gave away half his income to needy causes. There was so much demand from the poor for keepsake locks of his hair when he died that he was buried bald. Swift's grave is marked by a diamond shaped plaque and his epitaph is on the wall above him. Nearby are his death mask, a cast of his skull and a bust of the great man. You can also see a bookcase displaying early editions of Swift's work.

The cathedral's **stained-glass windows** date from the nineteenth century restoration – and here's something you probably don't know – the way to read a stained-glass window is from the bottom left-hand corner up. At the west end is Saint Patrick's window, telling his life story in thirty-nine images, from his kidnapping from Wales to his death.

St Pat's also acts as a memorial to Ireland's war dead – on display in the North Transept is an original copy of the **Roll of Honour**, an illustrated list of the fifty thousand Irish men and women who died in World War I.

At the top of the nave is a pew that the British royal family used in former times, identified by a carving of a lion and a unicorn. Among the bums that have graced this pew are those of Edward VI (son of Henry VIII), and Queen Victoria and Prince Albert. Nowadays this is reserved for the President of Ireland.

Behind the high altar is the small, but extensively renovated, **Lady Chapel**, built in 1270. It was once known as The French Chapel, after a bunch of French Huguenots had fled to Ireland when their Catholic compatriots started chopping them up. Among their descendants have been Nobel-prize-winning writer, **Samuel Beckett** and former Irish Taoiseach (Prime Minister), **Sean Lemass**.

Next door to the Cathedral is the attractive **St Patrick's Park**, which is the best place to get your snaps and, if it's a sunny day, to eat your sambos. Plaques honouring Ireland's great writers, such as Swift, Mangan, Wilde, Shaw, Yeats, Synge, O'Casey, Joyce, Dillon, Behan, Beckett, and Clarke, adorn the back wall – we churn out our literary geniuses in Ireland!

The Long Room of the Old Library, Trinity College Dublin

18. Trinity College

There's a popular joke in Trinity College that goes:
Question: What does a UCD (University College Dublin) student call a Trinity student after graduation?

Answer: Boss.

Yes, those deemed worthy to walk Trinity's hallowed halls like to consider themselves a cut above, and if you want evidence you can visit the students' Pav bar any night and watch them staggering around throwing up on each other in a very posh manner.

The history bit

But unlike the students, you're here to learn something. Such as the fact that if you were a Catholic, up until 1970 you would have faced excommunication for attending the university, as it was seen as a bastion of Protestantism. Luckily all that has changed now, as almost everyone attending Trinity is an atheist.

The Protestant thing all began back in 1592, when Queen Liz I, who referred to Ireland as *'that rude and barbarous nation'*, decided to try and civilise us. So, in between butchering our citizens and chopping people's heads off at court (and she called us barbarous?) Liz took time out to grant a royal charter for the establishment of a university.

The college expanded in subsequent centuries to become one of the world's most renowned seats of learning. It boasted such famed graduates as Jonathan Swift, Oscar Wilde, Bram Stoker (creator of Dracula), renowned philosophers George Berkeley and Edmund Burke, revered Irish nationalists Robert Emmet and Wolfe Tone, Nobel laureates Samuel Beckett (Literature), Ernest Walton (Physics) and Mairead Maguire (Peace), three Presidents of Ireland

and one Premier of New Zealand. And, of course, singer Chris de Burgh. But don't let that put you off.

Walking under the arch from College Green into **Parliament Square**, the first of the university's many quadrangles, is like stepping from a noisy modern city into an island of eighteenth-century peace, that's if you ignore all the students talking into iPhones. Directly ahead is the iconic **Campanile**, which has been towering over the college since 1853. Superstition holds that any student passing under it when the bell tolls will fail their exams. This superstition especially holds true for students who have spent the previous year missing lectures, getting rat-arsed and smoking pot.

One of the main reasons to visit Trinity is to see the **Old Library** and the **Book of Kells**. The library is entitled to a copy of every book published in Ireland or Britain every year, and it now has over five million books. Yes, even those with titles like *Nympho Psycho – The Return*. But you won't find that one in the Old Library, which holds the priceless Book of Kells, arguably the most valuable book in the world. It is a stunningly illuminated eighth-century version of the four Gospels and you may be interested to know that the ink was a mixture of soot and apple juice and the parchment was made from the skins of several hundred cows. The Book of Kells is undoubtedly Ireland's most viewed book.

The Library incorporates **The Long Room**, built in 1732. It's a stunning sixty-five-metre room with a vaulted ceiling, housing two hundred thousand old books. Among its treasures is one of the few surviving copies of the **1916 Proclamation of the Irish Republic**, which was read outside the GPO in 1916 by Patrick Pearse at the start of the Easter Rising. The Long Room also contains the **Brian Boru Harp**, although in all probability Brian Boru had been dead four hundred years when it was made. Brian, for your information, was the guy who defeated the Vikings in the Battle of Clontarf in 1014, where he met his end. The harp dates from the fifteenth century, and its left-facing image is the national symbol of Ireland, and more importantly, the right-facing image of the harp is the Guinness logo, with which fact you'll be boring people later in the pub.

Now go out and have a good wander around the place as there's lots more to see, like the fun **Science Gallery**,

Brian Boru's other harp

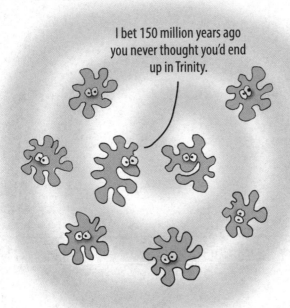

which features regularly changing and usually fascinating exhibitions, the wonderful and quirky **Douglas Hyde Gallery**, featuring contemporary art, **The Geological Museum**, where, among other things, you can see Mesozoic ostracods and Upper Palaeozoic miospores – try saying that when you've had six pints.

Trinity is almost always open to the public, it being a working university. But the best way to appreciate it is to take one of the entertaining tours, which happen every half hour, departing from just inside the main entrance. And having done all of that, you'll probably know more about Trinity College than most of the spotty-faced students.

The Jim Larkin statue and The Spire, O'Connell Street, Dublin

19. O'Connell Street and the GPO

In its time, poor O'Connell Street has been widened, narrowed, demolished, re-built, bombarded, re-built, bombarded again and re-built again. It has had three names and it has witnessed periods of splendour, tackiness, beauty, tragedy and glory. So if nothing else, it's interesting.

The history bit

The street was originally laid out as Drogheda Street in the seventeenth century and then widened in the mid-eighteenth century, when it was re-named Sackville Street after some lord who nobody in Ireland had ever heard of, and only extended to within about one hundred metres of the River Liffey. But in the late eighteenth century the street was extended to the river and, with the opening of the Carlisle Bridge (now **O'Connell Bridge**), business boomed – and it was regarded as one of the finest thoroughfares in the world.

The nineteenth century saw the building of many iconic structures such as The Palatial Mart (later the site of Clery's Department Store), the towering Nelson's Pillar (blown up), fine hotels like the Gresham and the Metropole and, of course, the GPO, or General Post Office. But we'll get to that.

At the street's southern end you'll see a fine statue of **Daniel O'Connell**, who won Catholic Emancipation back in

1829 by purely pacifist means. Four winged victories surround Dan, representing his virtues: Patriotism, Courage, Eloquence and Fidelity. Poor Courage has had a rough time of it – you can still see a bullet hole from the Rising in her right boob.

Another statue to look out for is the wonderfully expressive monument to **Jim Larkin**, the early twentieth-century trade union leader, which stands in the central median, almost directly opposite the GPO. It carries the inscription *'The great appear great because we are on our knees: Let us rise.'*

The site where the **Spire of Dublin** now stands was originally occupied by a forty-one-metre stone column, crowned with a statue of Admiral Nelson, which stood for one hundred and fifty years. In 1966, fifty years after the Rising, the IRA blew up the structure in the middle of the night without injuring a single Dubliner, one of the few humane achievements of the modern IRA.

The Spire, or the 'Erection at the Intersection', as Dubs have nicknamed it, is one hundred and twenty metres high. It was put up in 2003 and is supposed to represent something but nobody has a feckin' clue what.

Heading north from the Spire, there's a statue in the central median beyond the GPO, which might interest you if your itinerary includes getting rat-arsed in one of Dublin's fine pubs. It is that of **Father Theobald Mathew**, who was the man who essentially saved Ireland from drowning in a

sea of booze in the early nineteenth century. He managed to enrol three million people – half of Ireland's population at the time – into the Pioneer Total Abstinence Society. He was not a popular man with the breweries...

At the far north end of the street stands the impressive obelisk and statue to **Charles Stewart Parnell**, another legendary Irish nationalist leader of the late nineteenth century and one of those responsible for getting much of our land back from British landlords, which they'd simply nicked over the previous centuries.

The GPO

Now, imagine the scene. There you are on 24 April 1916, a lovely Easter Monday, strolling past the GPO, and the next thing you know, there are hordes of guys sticking guns in your face and proclaiming a free, independent Ireland. You see, the GPO is today one of the most iconic buildings in

Ireland, because it was chosen as the HQ for the Easter Rising, when Irish nationalists staged a revolt against British rule.

And they couldn't have chosen a finer building to watch being demolished about their heads. Built in 1818, it was one of the last great neo-classical buildings erected in Dublin. Sadly, the façade is all that remains of the original.

Anyway, back to the 1916 Rising. On that fateful Monday, about 1,200 armed rebels spread out to occupy key points around the city, with the GPO as their HQ. They removed the Union flag and replaced it with two Irish flags – one green with the words 'Irish Republic' and the other the Irish tricolour. Then the Rising's leader – Padraig Pearse – read aloud the Proclamation of the Irish Republic to the open-mouthed shoppers in front of the building.

The British were initially caught with their pants down – most of the officers were off gallivanting at the traditional Easter Monday race meeting in County Meath. As a result, the first troops they sent out took heavy casualties.

But for the lads in the GPO, it certainly wasn't any picnic. They came under heavy fire very soon, first from artillery behind barricades and then from the gunboat *Helga*, which the British had sent up the Liffey. Unfortunately, the gunner on the *Helga* left his glasses behind that morning and he managed to destroy most of the centre of Dublin, along with a great many of its citizens. After days of shelling, the GPO was, well, just a shell. The rebels surrendered after six days of fighting. Almost five hundred people lay dead and over two thousand were injured. Most of the leaders were executed. Up until then, the country had been sharply divided on the issue of British Rule, but after the executions (see Kilmainham Gaol), opinion swung sharply against the crown, which would lead ultimately to the Irish War of Independence three years later.

The GPO was finally restored in 1929 and became a symbol of Irish nationalism and heroism. Look out for the bullet holes in the main columns, which are still visible. A statue in the main foyer depicting the death of the Irish mythological hero, **Cú Chulainn** (pronounced *Ku-Kullen*) commemorates the Rising. As part of the Rising centenary commemoration, the GPO has opened a brand new **Witness History Museum**, which, according to the website, 'puts you right inside the GPO during Easter Week', but one presumes you won't have to dodge any bullets or explosions. Using all sorts of high-tech audio-visual yokes as well as

authentic artefacts, the museum offers you the chance to witness both sides of the conflict through the eyes of bystanders. You'll even get to declare the Irish Republic over the airwaves!

Attack of the property speculators

But if Dubs thought the British guns had done a lot of damage to O'Connell Street, they hadn't seen what city councillors and property speculators were capable of. For several decades up to the 1990s, they had a free-for-all, demolishing many fine buildings so they could provide us with much-needed burger joints and tacky amusement arcades. Thankfully, the street has undergone a renaissance in recent years, with much of the tat removed, the paths widened, traffic reduced, new street furnishings and sculpture and the protection of what's left of the street's architectural heritage.

Shops and other stuff

The landmark shop on O'Connell Street was **Clery's Department Store**, almost opposite the GPO. The business began in 1853 and the original building was flattened during the Rising. The present fine building dates from the 1920s, but sadly the famous shop went out of business in 2015. The Clery's clock was a well-known meeting point for Dubs, particularly for a romantic rendezvous, and hopefully a quick snog.

If you're facing the GPO, the street on the right leading off O'Connell Street is **Henry Street**, the most popular shopping street in Dublin. It is considered a kind of downmarket version of Grafton Street, but usually only by snobby eejits. It is an interesting street do a bit of shopping, and it will probably cost you a few bob less. About a hundred metres along on the right, you'll see **Moore Street**, famed as the place where the rebels finally surrendered in 1916, and also an iconic Dublin fruit and veg market. Moore Street is usually very busy and colourful, with lots of stalls overflowing with apples, peaches and sticks of celery, in case you're in a healthy diet frame of mind. Much of the street's colour comes from the sellers themselves, who are usually hardworking ladies with thick Dublin accents shouting things like 'Gedyerorngesforforayouro' ('Get your oranges four for a euro.')

A word of warning. After dark, and particularly late at night, O'Connell Street may become a bit rough, with all sorts of drunken eejits and drug-addled gougers staggering around. The smart thing to do, obviously, is avoid it at night, but by all means don't miss it during daylight hours.

The interior of Kilmainham Gaol, Dublin

20. Kilmainham Gaol

No visit to Dublin is complete without spending some time in one of its prisons, though hopefully not because you ran down O'Connell Street in the nip. To be specific, a visit to Kilmainham Gaol is a must for anyone with an interest in the past, and in particular, Ireland's struggle for independence. It's a most rewarding couple of hours.

The history bit

The gaol was built in 1796 at a site known as Gallows Hill. With the hill and tree for stringing up offenders obliterated by the edifice, a new-fangled drop platform was erected on the balcony above the entrance. At the time, there was an execution every couple of months. And it was in public, naturally, so the whole family could enjoy a nice outing and watch some poor gouger have his neck stretched. Hangings were eventually relocated to a room within the walls.

Kilmainham's early days were pretty squalid, with no segregation for prisoners. Men, women and children were often crammed five to a cell, and the prison's youngest inmate was aged seven. Kids were usually put in prison for stuff like stealing a loaf of bread.

Architecturally, the most impressive bit is the East or Victorian Wing, which features a large, barrel-vaulted space with iron galleries and catwalks, lit by a huge skylight. The design afforded the guard a perfect 270-degree view. The amazing acoustics also allowed a guard to hear any hanky-panky in the cells, such as someone ordering out for a pizza.

In the slammer...

As soon as you enter the building, you get a sense of the conditions. It is full of narrow, dank and dark corridors and shadowy nooks and crannies. Most cells are locked, but you can peer through spy holes in the doors and imagine a bunch of poor feckers inside lying about on straw. You will also have the opportunity to enter a cell and have the door slammed behind you, thus catering for the masochistic.

But the real reason Kilmainham is a shrine in Irish consciousness is because it housed, at one time or another, a vast array of major figures from the struggle for Irish freedom, and especially those associated with the 1916 Rising. Hardly had the place opened when it took delivery of the leaders of the 1798 rebellion, quickly followed by those of the 1803 rebellion, 1848, 1867, 1916, the War of Independence (1919–21) and finally the Civil War (1922–23). The list of inmates reads like a 'Who's Who of Irish History':

1803: Michael Dwyer – One of the 1798 rebellion's leaders, who waged a guerrilla war against the British in County Wicklow.

1803: Robert Emmet – leader of the 1803 Rebellion. Hanged, drawn and quartered.

1867: Jeremiah O'Donovan Rossa – Legendary Irish Fenian leader.

1881: Charles Stewart Parnell – Renowned statesman who campaigned for Irish land reform and Home Rule.

1881: Michael Davitt – Founder of the Irish National Land League.

1916: Leaders of the Easter Rising.

Charles Stewart Parnell, who was from a terribly posh background, was arrested for his land-reform activities. While in Kilmainham, he was allowed the luxuries to which he was accustomed, and a contemporary drawing shows him sitting in a comfy armchair chatting to a lady friend before a blazing fire. Such was his stature that the British Government negotiated with him in prison, resulting in

Sorry to disturb, Mister Parnell, but here's more coal for your fire.

'The Kilmainham Treaty', which won major concessions for Irish tenant farmers.

Kilmainham's most famous prisoners were the leaders of the 1916 Easter Rising. After the Rising, The British sentenced ninety men to death. Fourteen were ultimately executed by firing squad in the Stonebreakers' Yard, including the seven signatories of the Proclamation of the Irish Republic: Padraig Pearse, Thomas J Clarke, Sean Mac Diarmada, Thomas Mac Donagh, Eamonn Ceannt, James Connolly and Joseph Plunkett, would subsequently become legendary figures for what many saw as their 'blood sacrifice'. A striking sculpture representing those executed, complete with bullet holes, stands across the road from the gaol.

During the War of Independence (1919–21), hundreds of prisoners were held here and then, in the Civil War (1922–23), the Free State Government incarcerated hundreds of anti-Treaty soldiers. It was during this period that a curious incident happened in the gaol. Upon hearing of the death of Michael Collins, who was the Republicans' former leader in the War of Independence but who was now their enemy, seven hundred of the prisoners fell to their knees and said a rosary in his honour, such was the reverence in which Collins was held.

Collins's principal adversary in the Civil War, Eamon de Valera, who would be a major figure in Irish politics for the next five decades, and future President of Ireland, was the last prisoner to be held in Kilmainham Gaol, and the doors finally banged shut for the last time in 1924. Thanks be to Jaysus.

Undying love

One of the most moving experiences of the gaol tour is the account of the last hours of one of the leaders of the Easter Rising, Joseph Plunkett, and his fiancée, Grace Gifford, who were married in the tiny Kilmainham chapel under the watchful eyes of twenty British soldiers. Afterwards, Plunkett was immediately taken away, although they were granted ten minutes together in his cell later that day, again under the watchful eye of soldiers. Seven hours after his marriage, he was shot. Grace never married again.

Glasnevin Cemetery, Dublin

21. Glasnevin Cemetery and Museum

I did not come to Dublin to spend my time wandering around a bunch of old graves in a f***ing cemetery!'

Yes, we can just hear the argument when the other half makes the suggestion. As far as you're concerned, the next time you go to a cemetery, you'll be in box. This is a grave error. (Geddit?) Besides being a totally fascinating and moving place, Glasnevin also gives us the opportunity to indulge in some deadly puns. Trust us, people have been dying to get into Glasnevin for centuries.

Glasnevin Cemetery's list of residents reads like a who's who of Irish history, political and social, and you could easily bury yourself in the many fascinating stories about the ordinary folk who are pushing up daisies here. The place is a national monument and the museum is really engrossing – it won a European Museum of the Year award in 2012. It will really bring the entire place to life for you.

The history bit

Back in the early nineteenth century, the Catholic Irish had nowhere to bury their dead, so Catholics had to be buried in Protestant cemeteries with little or no religious service. Step up Daniel O'Connell (see O'Connell Street), who used his influence to force the opening of a cemetery for all religions. Glasnevin opened on 21 February 1832, complete with a high wall and watchtowers to deter despicable body snatchers. The first burial was of eleven-year-old Michael Carey from a poverty-stricken area of inner Dublin. Around 1.5 million people have taken up permanent residence since, and some of the most interesting tales concern the ordinary people of Dublin and beyond.

One such tale concerned the cholera victims who were buried here in the nineteenth century who, from beyond the grave, ended up giving cholera to loads of other people down the road because their bodies infected the water source. Or the baby who was killed in crossfire during the 1916 Rising and, because of martial law, had to be buried

at 7am with only his grandfather present. Or the heart-breaking Little Angels' plot, which contains 50,000 babies who were mostly stillborn – Glasnevin was the only cemetery that allowed burials of unbaptised babies in consecrated ground. There are a million other fascinating tales waiting to be dug up. So stop looking like you're going to a funeral.

Glasnevin Cemetery Museum

This is a rare thing indeed – a beautiful piece of modern architecture. It includes a visitor centre, crypt museum, restaurant, exhibition space, the Daniel O'Connell lecture hall and also has a high-tech genealogy section. So, if you think you've a bit of Irish in you, here's your chance to track down any possible ancestors who have a connection with Glasnevin. The fanciest gadget in the museum is the ten-metre-long, interactive timeline, which contains the stories of two hundred of the most interesting stiffs.

The City of the Dead is not a Hollywood zombie movie, but an exhibition telling the stories of gravediggers, body snatchers, burial practices and old and new religious beliefs associated with death and burial.

But the best way to see Glasnevin is to take one of the **guided tours**, which are really interesting and not without humour, believe it or not. But in the meantime, here's a sneak preview of some of the dead famous inhabitants.

Daniel O'Connell

The largest and most elaborate mausoleum in the cemetery, the round tower can be spotted the moment you arrive. It's over 50 metres tall and based on the round towers built by ancient Irish monks. Daniel O'Connell, one of the greatest reforming figures in Irish history, died in Genoa in 1847 while on a pilgrimage, and his heart was taken to Rome and the rest of him sent back to Ireland. O'Connell's coffin can be seen and touched through portals cut into the marble surround. Loyalist terrorists tried to blow up the tower in 1971, but the gobshites only succeeded in making a noise loud enough to wake the dead.

Charles Stewart Parnell

'The Uncrowned King of Ireland', as he was known, Parnell was the man who brought about a massive agrarian transformation, returning much of the land to us that had been nicked by the Brits. He also brought Ireland to the brink of Home Rule. He was only 45 when he died of a heart attack. He wanted his grave to be a simple affair and it is – a grass mound marked only by a large boulder taken from his home county, Wicklow. Two hundred thousand people attended the funeral – so many that it took them until after dark to reach the cemetery.

Michael Collins

'The Big Fellow', as he was known, was one of the men most responsible for Ireland's independence, leading a guerrilla war against the British from 1919 to 1921, until the British eventually signed a treaty that offered a qualified independence – but also led to the partition of Ireland. That led to the Irish Civil War during which Collins was tragically assassinated. He was only 31. If you thought Parnell's funeral was well attended, Big Mick's brought five hundred thousand people out. His grave is a relatively simple one, right behind the cemetery museum. Fresh flowers are a permanent feature. In 1922, when Collins arrived at Dublin Castle to accept the handover of power, the British leader remarked angrily that Collins was seven minutes late, to which The Big Fellow calmly replied: 'We've been waiting over 700 years, you can have the extra seven minutes'.

Jeremiah O'Donovan Rossa

The Fenian leader died in 1915, having spent much of his life in exile in America. His grave is best known as the place where the leader of the 1916 Rising, Padraig Pearse, made his graveside oration, one of the most famous speeches in Irish history. If you happen to be doing a tour at 2.30pm (Mar–Sept), you'll be lucky enough to catch an actor playing the role of Pearse deliver the famed lines:

> 'They think that they have pacified Ireland. They think that they have purchased half of us and intimidated the other half. They think that they have foreseen everything: but the fools, the fools, the fools! – they have left us our Fenian dead, and while Ireland holds these graves, Ireland unfree shall never be at peace!'

Watch the Irish chests swell with pride...

Is this going to be dead boring or dead interesting?

GLASNEVIN TOURS

And they're just a sampler. There are a hundred other graves of interest and even some of the graves of people you've never heard of are fascinating – some of them are larger than your house!

Kylemore Lough and the Twelve Bens, Connemara, County Galway

22. Connemara National Park

It's hard to define where exactly Connemara starts and ends, but it's roughly the area of about 400 sq km to the west and northwest of Galway. Connemara National Park is a teensy bit of this, at 30 sq km, but is completely free of development and contains a gansey-load of breathtaking scenery. And you'll enjoy it all the more if you pack your walking shoes.

So what's there? Well, there's a **Visitor Centre** with exhibitions about the local flora, fauna and geology. It also has a tearoom, picnic tables, cute Connemara ponies and even a playground, in case you fancy a go on a see-saw. There are also, naturally, walking trails, and these are the real reason to visit the park. Get out and blow off the cobwebs!

The park is largely centred around **Diamond Hill** (sorry, no diamonds here!), the origin of that name lost in the Connemara mists, although it might come from the peak-shaped summit, which makes it look sort-of diamondy, if you use your imagination. Whatever about that, the views from the slopes and particularly the summit are priceless. There's a selection of tracks to suit everyone from the slob-like doss-artist, to the energetic summiteer. There are also some interesting **megalithic court tombs** (tombs with a burial chamber) in the park that date back four thousand years. In the Visitor Centre, you'll find information on all of the historical stuff to see. Make sure you bring some rain gear, even on sunny days – it can change from clear blue skies to Arctic tundra quicker than you can say 'my feckin' legs are banjaxed!'

Oh, and the good news is that entry is FREE!

OK, maybe we didn't need to bring a see-saw.

Kylemore Abbey and Kylemore Lough, Connemara, County Galway

23. Kylemore Abbey

Kylemore Abbey looks like it was lifted straight out of a Harry Potter novel, or might even double as a location for Castle Dracula – yes, the building and setting are quite stunning, and the surrounding estate a mecca for walkers and nature-lovers.

Set on the shores of Pollacappal Lough with Doughruagh Mountain's steep, afforested slops rising behind it, the Abbey was built by a wealthy doctor, Mitchell Henry, who, when he wasn't treating runny noses, piles and varicose veins, was busy getting rich in the textile business. He had the castle (as it was known then) built in 1867 as a gesture of love for his wife Margaret. Isn't that sweet? In 1920, a murmur of Benedictine nuns (yes, that's the collective noun for nuns!) took over the castle and turned it into a boarding school, which operated until 2010.

Besides the Abbey, the estate also boasts a beautiful neo-Gothic church, a glorious walled garden and a ganseyload of woodland and lakeshore walks. You can't visit the entire Abbey, but your ticket gives you access to a bunch of beautifully restored rooms on the ground floor. There are guided tours daily, which will fill you in on all the interesting bits n' bobs about the estate's history and the local legends. And a trio of eateries in and about the estate serve lots of great Irish nosh, which you'll no doubt enjoy after all that wearying woodland strolling.

People walking through Shop Street in Galway city

24. Shop Street, Galway

Guess what you'll find on Shop Street? Yep, you got it. Shops. All sorts of shops. Book shops, clothes shops, craft shops, shoe shops, jewellery shops, music shops, souvenir shops...well, you get the idea. But perhaps the best thing on offer in the area that's roughly between Eyre Square and the River Corrib is the atmosphere, or as Galwegians might describe it, the craic! Shop Street sits at the centre of a collection of lovely narrow streets that follow a medieval pattern, among them William Street, High Street, Middle Street and Quay Street – it's like Galway's 'Latin Quarter'.

Besides the shopping, you'll find a load of great pubs and restaurants, several with patio seating so you can enjoy your pint and sandwich in the bucketing rain! The eclectic mix of traders is mirrored in the mix of brightly coloured buildings and there are also some older, more historical gems, some of which have been refurbished as shops and businesses.

Watch for **Lynch's Castle** where William Street becomes Shop Street. It's a bank now but it was built in the sixteenth century by the powerful Lynch clan. And here's a morbid but interesting little tale...in 1493, the chief magistrate of Galway, James Lynch FitzStephen, hanged his own son from the window of his home for murdering a Spanish sailor. It wasn't from this building but one in Market Street next to **St Nicholas' Church**, and part of the house and the hanging window survive. It's been claimed that this is the origin of the term 'lynching'. It makes for a nice, gruesome pic opportunity. Also keep an eye out for a lovely statue on William Street of **Oscar Wilde** conversing with Estonian writer Eduard Wilde, although the pair never met.

I'd like to buy some of your finest craic, please.

All in all, there's plenty to savour on Shop Street and thereabouts without actually doing any shopping!

Looking down Inis Mór's coastline to the Atlantic

25. The Aran Islands

Perhaps the last outpost of Irish culture in its purest form. The islands' near complete isolation from the modern world lasted until just a few decades ago and many of the traditions and the language, from that time survive. All the islanders still speak Gaelic, there's a refreshing lack of modern life's trappings, a desolate, inspiring, and largely untouched landscape, impressive ancient forts and monastic ruins, genuine traditional music, some thatched cottages and crafts unique to the islands. As *National*

Geographic put it, 'That this feeling, this authenticity, has survived the modern world is nothing short of miraculous.' So leave your watch behind, turn off your mobile phone and step back into a simpler world on the three islands of Inis Mór (Inishmore, Big Island), Inis Meáin (Inishmaan, Middle Island) and Inis Oírr (Inisheer, East Island).

The history bit

There have been people here for five thousand years and they left their mark in the form of megalithic tombs. But we'll get to that. During the late Bronze Age and through the Iron Age (roughly 1100 BC to AD 500), the islanders built large stone forts, and some of these survive largely intact. But we'll get to that as well.

Next up came the Christians. St Enda founded the first monastic settlements in the fifth century, and ruins from the eighth century are still fending off the Atlantic storms.

The Gaelic clan of the O'Briens laid claim to the islands in the thirteenth century and left behind a castle on Inis Oírr. But in 1582 along came the O'Flahertys, who hacked a few O'Briens into bits. There are still many (peaceful!) O'Briens and O'Flahertys on the islands today – direct descendants of these people.

Cromwell's murderous forces seized the islands in 1652 and built a garrison. During the Great Famine (1845–51), the islands fared better than most thanks to the plentiful fishing grounds surrounding them, but like in the rest of

Ireland, English absentee landlords owned the infertile land and extracted exorbitant rents, though we've long since kicked their greedy arses out! And that was a long time ago, so no hard feelings to our English friends!

The bits to see

The most impressive of the stone forts is **Dún Aengus** (*dún* means fort in Irish, BTW). It is semi-circular and sits on the edge of a precipice plunging one hundred metres to the Atlantic. It was built between 1100 and 500 BC and consists of an inner court fifty metres across surrounded by a wall six metres high and five metres thick. Outside is a rampart known as a 'cheval-de-frise' – a scary-looking field of sharp, upward-pointing rocks, the idea being to impale attackers and turn their insides into their outsides. The ruins also feature a huge rectangular stone slab, although nobody really knows what it was, but one can imagine all sorts of nasty sacrificial things. Again the experts are uncertain why Dún Aengus has its D-shape. It may have been deliberate or it may have once been circular and the other half has collapsed into the Atlantic. Just be careful near the edge especially on windy days. Dún Aengus is one of the finest prehistoric monuments in Europe, and is currently seeking the UNESCO World Heritage stamp of approval, which it clearly deserves.

Dún Dúchathair sits on a spectacular rocky promontory, stretching out into the sea, thanks to the Atlantic having battered the bejaysus out of the land on either side. On its outer side there are walls six metres high and five metres wide.

There are two other large stone forts on Inis Mór at **Dún Eochla** and **Dún Eoghanachta**, and there are loads of small forts. The only one where an excavation has been carried out is Dún Aengus, but they're all worth checking out.

Teampall Bheanáin is a good place to say a little prayer, considering it is the smallest church in the world! Or so they say. It dates from the eleventh century and besides the missing roof, looks exactly as it did yonks ago.

Teampall Chiaráin is in the village of Mainistir and was founded in the twelfth century. Several cross-decorated slabs are nearby, the most striking with a hole, indicating it may have been used as a sundial. The tradition is to draw a cloth through the hole and bring the blessing of

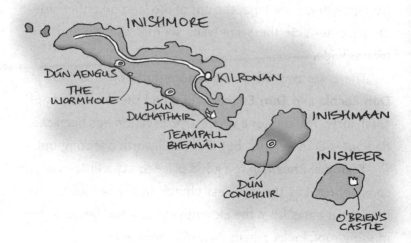

fertility. So if you're looking to get preggers, get your hanky or scarf ready!

The **Puffing Holes** are clifftop, tunnel-like channels down to the ocean. Any time there are decent waves, water creates a jet like that of a gigantic whale's blowhole. Great craic altogether!

The Wormhole or Poll na bPéist, is a striking natural rock formation near Dún Aengus. The water rushes into the large rectangular Wormhole through an underground cave, or when the waves are big, spills over and fills it up from above.

Hopping over to **Inis Meáin** you'll discover the largest, at seventy-nine metres, of all the Aran forts in **Dún Crocbhur**, which sits near the island's highest point. It's a magnificent structure with an equally magnificent view of the landscape and its patchwork of stone-walled fields. And

136

there are a couple of pubs within walking distance!

WB Yeats, James Joyce, John Millington Synge and Colm Tóibín were all inspired by the starkly beautiful and remote Inis Meáin. Many of the leaders of Ireland's Easter Rising also came here to immerse themselves in the culture before the rebellion. Synge was a playwright and poet whose masterpieces *The Playboy of the Western World* and *The Well of the Saints* found much of their inspiration in the people of the Aran Islands. **Synge's Cottage** is a pretty, thatched building and is now a small museum that's open in summer.

Hopping over to **Inis Oirr**, wherever you are on the island, you'll never be far from **O'Brien's Castle**. Built in 1585, this tower house was constructed within the remains of an ancient ring fort called **Dún Formna**. You can wander about the ruins and take nice snaps of the golden beach and harbour below.

The Aran jumper

This is not a type of Irish kangaroo. If you're American, you probably know these as 'sweaters'. And to Irish speakers, it's a geansaí (pronounced gan-zee). Aran jumpers are known the world over and are always in fashion. The original jumpers were made with coarse sheep's wool that retained the natural oils. This made them largely waterproof, which was handy in a place where it rains 364 days a year! Traditional Aran jumpers have a thick, interwoven cable pattern and are off-white in colour. The particular stitches in an Aran jumper are said to be reflection of the lives of the knitters and are sometimes associated with a particular clan.

Best foot forward...

Getting around is best achieved by leg-power i.e. on a bike or on your own two feet. You can hire bikes on all three islands and there's a bike to suit bums of all shapes and sizes. It's the best way to explore, and you'll get plenty of fresh air and exercise.

Then there's the walking option – plan a long walk, perhaps a day or half a day, and you'll probably be able to take in most of the sights and scenery. Just wandering the boreens (laneways) is inspiring, marvelling at the rock-walled fields that have been there for centuries. So get your lazy arse moving and get the most from your visit.

Part of any Aran Islands visit is to immerse yourself in the local lingo and tradition. So, instead of always speaking English, French, German or Kaixana, how about learning a few handy Gaelic phrases? The locals will appreciate your efforts:

Hello (to one person) – Dia duit (Dee-a-git)
Hello (to more than one person) – Dia daoibh (Dee-a-give)
Goodbye – Slán! (Slawn)
Goodbye for now – Slán go fóill! (Slawn-guh-fole)
Thank you – Go raibh maith agat (Guh-rev-mah-a-gut)
I love you – Tá grá agam duit (Tah-grah-agum-dit)
I'd like to buy some sun block please – Ba mhaith liom buío-

chas a cheannach bloc ghrian le do thoil. (Buh-wha-lum-bwee-chus-a-chian-ach-bloc-green-le-duh-hull)

Tá grá agam duit.   Slán!

(But don't worry, you'll never need the last phrase – we guarantee it!)

Don't stop at the lingo. Go along to the many pubs that host trad music sessions. You'll soon find your foot tapping away by itself completely independently of your brain.

Island hopping

Each island has its own unique characteristics and sights. Inis Oírr, for example has a population of just two hundred and fifty – that's fewer people than Jennifer Lopez hires to do her hair. Inis Meáin, although larger, has only two hundred islanders and is the least trodden by tourists. There are regular ferries connecting all three islands.

But we'll leave you with the words of WB Yeats, who, when giving advice to JM Synge on finding inspiration, said:

'Go to the Aran Islands. Live there as if you were one of the people themselves. Express a life that never before has found expression.'

Slea Head, Dingle Peninsula, County Kerry

26. The Dingle Peninsula

This fabulous finger of mountainous land juts out into the Atlantic Ocean and was once described by *National Geographic* as the most beautiful place on Earth. And it's hard to argue with that. But besides the scenery, there's the history – at over two thousand sites, spanning six thousand years, the peninsula has the highest density of archaeological monuments in Europe. And to help you rest your historically engorged brain, Dingle has a gazillion welcoming, hostelries. Sure, why would you ever want to leave?

Hit the road

Pretty much any road you choose to drive will constitute a scenic drive, but if you're looking for a starting point, take the N86 out of Tralee towards Dingle town, passing the lovely **Blennerville Windmill**, and hugging the north coast. After about 15 km the road veers left through the mountains, and there's scenery you could eat all the way. If you can, take a break at the **South Pole Inn** in the sleepy village of **Annus-**

You get a great pint in The South Pole Inn.

caul. The pub is so called because it was opened by Tom Crean, a famed Antarctic explorer, and there's also a statue of the man in the town. Continue along the N86, passing some more fierce savage views until you reach Dingle.

Dingle is a lovely little place, famed for its friendliness, its charming cosmopolitanism, and its fish! The village offers an eclectic mix of craft shops, galleries, bookshops and other interesting bits and bobs. There are a bunch of great pubs and restaurants, many of them with fish so fresh it would almost talk to you from the plate. It's also had a famed visitor for over thirty years – Fungie the Dolphin. He's been hanging about the harbour since 1983 and is so friendly that he almost always obliges when boats take tourists out to see him. In fact, a bunch of people are probably going to go broke when Fungie finally kicks the bucket! There's even a statue of him!

Take the **Slea Head** drive (R559) west from the town. If you thought the views before were good, then hold on to your seat, because this looping drive of about 50 km is

This is almost as good as Dingle Oceanworld.

beyond breath-taking. You'll know you've reached Slea Head when you see a shrine with a white cross. The spot also provides fab views of **The Blasket Islands**, and, if you can, try to make the time to visit Great Blasket, which was inhabited up to the 1950s by a completely Irish-speaking population and is jammers with history, birdlife and scenery. The road continues around through more luscious landscape all the way back to Dingle, but you're not done yet, because the return journey to Tralee takes you through the **Conor Pass** and more spell-binding views all the way home.

But don't stick to the main roads – explore! Some of the lesser-travelled by-ways will take you to wonderful beaches, such as the ironically named 5-km **Inch Strand**. Other roads will take you back in time, such as **Reask Monastic Site**, **Gallarus Oratory and Castle** or **Dúnbeg Fort**.

One last thing. Most of the west of the peninsula is a Gaeltacht area, meaning Irish is spoken, but don't worry, everyone also speaks English. Of course if you're Uzbekistani, you're s*** out of luck.

Skellig Michael from the mainland

27. Skellig Michael

I f you're lucky enough to visit this spectacular monument to nature's beauty and man's ingenuity and dedication, you will need the following: rain gear, walking boots or shoes, a camera, an empty bladder, a head for heights, legs capable of climbing hundreds of steep steps. Oh, and a light sabre. Or at least that's what recent visitors have been bringing along and then snapping each other pretending to be Luke Skywalker, because parts of *Star Wars* were filmed here.

The thing is that once you actually ascend the steps to the monastery and get a sense of the awesome natural and man-made majesty, the *Star Wars* stuff will be quickly forgotten, as no movie can convey the emotional punch of the place. Yep, Skellig Michael is that feckin' good.

The history bit

The islands first appear in Irish legend in 1400 BC when a Milesian ship supposedly foundered on the rocks, killing the son of Milesius, called Ir, who promptly buried him there. The Milesians were supposedly the last race to settle Ireland, driving the Tuatha Dé Danann, a supernatural race, below ground, although these keep popping up every now and then as fairies or leprechauns. Never knew that, did you?

The first definite reference to monks on the Skelligs dates to the eighth century when the death of 'Suibhni of Scelig' is recorded. The ascetic monks who built the monastery installed an impressive three sets of steps, many of which are literally carved from the rocks. They came here to escape the world of men and be one with God, and they lived largely on fish, not surprisingly, birds' eggs and a few veggies. Their life was incredibly harsh, especially in winter, and you had to hand it to these boyos, they were tough as old boots, not that they had the luxury of those.

Inevitably, the smelly, murderous Vikings showed up. In 824 'Scelec was plundered by the heathens, and Etgal (the abbot) was carried off into captivity.' But those monks were anything if not forgiving, and persuasive, because in 993, the great Viking leader, Olav Trygvasson, who later became King of Norway, was baptised by a hermit on Skellig Michael and went home to introduce Christianity to his country.

The islands' dedication to Saint Michael the Archangel appears to have happened some time before 1044 when the death of 'Aedh of Scelic-Mhichál' was recorded.

The monastery was continuously occupied by about twelve or so monks until the thirteenth century, when there was a shift in climate, the temperate dropped and the storms became more powerful. So, after five or six centuries, they packed their goatskins and headed for the mainland. The Irish Government purchased the island in 1989, and it became a UNESCO World Heritage Site in 1996. And then Luke Skywalker showed up...

The bits to see

The Skelligs comprise two islands, **Skellig Michael** (or Great Skellig) and **Little Skellig**, the former inhabited by tourists and birds, the latter only by birds. The islands are about 15 km off County Kerry. Skellig Michael soars precipitously like a great natural pyramid from the Atlantic Ocean to two hundred and eighteen metres. It's just fifty-four acres in area at its base. There are actually two distinct peaks, and just below the lower one, about one hundred and eighty metres up, you'll find the remains of the **monastery**, once

I can't help feeling it's against the spirit of things.

the most westerly Christian settlement in Europe, consisting of six beehive cells, two oratories, a medieval church and lots of ancient stone crosses and graves, all enclosed by high walls. There's also a hermitage clinging precariously to the cliffs, just for any of the monks who didn't feel isolated enough.

But first there's the boat crossing, which can be rough, so don't eat a full Irish breakfast just before embarking. The scenery on the way out is wonderful, especially as you approach the islands and Skellig Michael towers above you, a great pinnacle of rock with splashes of green speckling its crevices. The views back towards the mainland are also quite stunning.

You have some hard work ahead as you ascend. There are **six hundred and seventy steps** and the climb is very steep, so as an excuse you should pause every now and then and pretend to admire the monks' amazing masonry skills, while your heart pumps at two hundred beats a minute and your lungs are screaming for mercy. When it's wet, the steps can be slippery and there are no handrails – seriously, people have been blown away, literally, over a cliff, so be careful.

When you reach the top and pass through a monastery's enclosing walls, you'll see a cluster of small, ancient buildings. On the left are the six monks' cells, known as 'beehive cells' or 'clocháns', built using a dry stone method. They have corbelled roofs, which means, just in case you haven't a bog's notion, that one rock is placed on top of the other projecting slightly in, so that the roof slopes up to a point. The huts look just like somewhere you'd expect to find an ascetic monk. Or a Jedi Knight for that matter.

On the right is the medieval St Michael's Church, and behind that an oratory and the monks' burial ground. Further along, separate from the rest of the buildings, is the second oratory. All of the above is perched on a cliff face overlooking the endless sweep of the Atlantic.

A bird's eye view

The other thing to see on Skellig Michael is, of course, the birdlife. Little Skellig is home to a colony of twenty thousand gannets, making it arguably the largest colony on Earth.

FASQ (Frequently Asked Stupid Questions)

Are there toilets on the island?
The idea is to keep the place as it was a thousand years ago and as the monks used the facilities provided by nature, you'll have to do the same. So a big NO.

Are there dining facilities there?
Only if you like raw fish or seaweed.

Can I bring my own food?
By all means, but if you leave any rubbish behind, offenders may be legally thrown from a cliff – after they've picked up their litter. And you can't stop for your picnic in the actual monastic site. Otherwise, munch away.

What about a souvenir shop?
Yeah, sure, you can buy plastic Luke Skywalkers and light sabres, along with 'I'm a Skellig Jedi' T-shirts. And if you haven't detected the sarcasm, you must be a right eejit.

Are there guides on the island?
Actually, yes, there are friendly folk there to answer all your questions, such as 'how many faces does a dodecahedron have?' Actually, we jest, but they should be able to speak with authority on all aspects of the monastic site.

There are a bunch of private operators who ferry people to the island from May to October, departing mostly from **Ballinskelligs Pier** or **Portmagee**. But even if you've booked in advance, your trip might be cancelled if weather doesn't permit. Damn inconsiderate nature!

Ross Castle on the edge of Killarney's lower lake

28. The Ring of Kerry

No, it's not like the one in *Lord of the Rings*, with magical powers that turn you into a leprechaun or something. On the other hand, many of its magical attractions will leave you with precious memories.

The Ring is a wonderful route of 179 km around the fringes of County Kerry's Iveragh Peninsula. It weaves a beautiful path through stunning scenery, pretty villages, historic sites, and 'craic agus ceol' galore. That literally means 'fun and music' (pronounced: krahk ah-gus ky-ohl), but a better translation would be 'fun, conversation, drinking, carousing and music.'

Officially the starting point is Killarney, but it's entirely up to you. The advice is to travel the Ring anti-clockwise to minimise traffic congestion; tour buses are obliged to travel anti-clockwise. And one other thing – don't just stick to the main Ring road. Wander off into the middle and explore some of the roads untravelled by tour buses, otherwise you'll miss a lot of really deadly stuff.

So, moving in the recommended anti-clockwise direction, here are a bunch of places you'll encounter on your odyssey around the world famous Ring of Kerry.

Killarney

The unofficial 'capital' of the Ring of Kerry, Killarney is a mecca for tourists, jammers with great pubs, restaurants and enough welcoming hotels and guesthouses to cater for Atilla the Hun's invading armies. It's a large town by Kerry standards, and it's a pretty town in its own right.

The town sits right on the edge of Killarney National Park, a UNESCO Biosphere Reserve. It's a stunningly beautiful area of 102 sq km, which is jam-packed with lakes, mountains, forests, wildlife and history. Strictly speaking, if you follow the anti-clockwise direction of the Ring, you should wait until the return journey before exploring it. But to hell with that! Take the car, bike, horse, or just use your legs and hike and go wandering into the hills south along the N71 road.

Your first stop should be **Ross Castle**, the medieval home to the Irish chieftain, O'Donoghue Mór. You'll see a sign for it just as you leave town. The castle sits in a majestic setting on the shores of **Lough Leane**, with Ireland's highest mountains, **The Macgillycuddy Reeks** rising in the distance behind it.

You can also visit **Innisfallen Island** from Ross Castle. The small island contains the impressive ruins of an extensive twelfth-century **Augustinian priory** and a small eleventh-century **Romanesque church**. Local boatmen arrange trips, which take only a few minutes.

Back on the road and a bit further along is **Muckross Abbey** and **Muckross House and Gardens**. Both are well worth a visit. Queen Victoria and Prince Albert stayed here. The Abbey is a fifteenth-century ruin with a cloistered

Not the kind of waterfall I was hoping for.

TORC WATERFALL

courtyard and a giant yew tree growing in the middle. The Tudor-style house nearby was built in the nineteenth century and its gardens will make your own attempt back home look like a garbage tip by comparison.

Next stop is **Torc Waterfall**. It's not exactly the Zambezi Falls, but its woodland setting makes it very pretty indeed. And there are lots of walking trails if you are so inclined.

As you continue your travels, the road starts to meander and rise quite steeply. With the lush woodlands behind you, an entrancing, majestic landscape unfolds. There are so many photo ops you'll probably need to post to Facebook that you're about to crash their server.

We'll make our last stop on this bit at **'Ladies' View'**.

The story goes that when Queen Victoria visited Killarney in 1861, her ladies-in-waiting did a recce of the area and decided that this particular spot was the most beautiful, fit for a queen, in fact. It's actually fit for any eyes that appreciate natural majesty.

The road continues up to Moll's Gap, and it is surely one of the most beautiful in the world. But we'll return to it from the other direction. Now it's time to turn anticlockwise again and resume our Ring exploration.

The Gap of Dunloe

Follow the N72 west until you see a sign for the **Gap of Dunloe**. The road is narrow and winding, and usually busy in the summer. It's also a popular route for jaunting cars, so expect to get stuck behind one and don't get mad – relax and use the opportunity to take in the scenery.

Near the beginning of the ascent to the Gap, you'll come to **Kate Kearney's Cottage**. Kate was a real looker, by all accounts, and used to make poitín, or illicit spirit, back in the day, which was said to be 'very fierce and wild', meaning you could probably use it to fuel an interstellar rocket. Anyway, the cottage has long since been turned into a family business, and there's a pub, restaurant and gift shop.

Continue past the cottage and simply enjoy the natural grandeur of the Gap road, which continues for about 7 km rising through 200 m and passing four beautiful loughs.

There's loads more great scenery beyond the Gap,

which we recommend you explore if you've time. But our Ring exploration resumes back down on the N72.

Killorglin

The pretty enough little town of Killorglin sits on the beautiful **River Laune**, which you'll cross on the way in. You may have spotted a statue of a goat with a crown perched on a rock at the eastern end of the bridge. This is not some local madness like Caligula appointing his horse to the Roman Senate. Instead, it's a very good excuse for the mother of all parties. The story goes that when the murderous, vicious Cromwellian forces (we *really* don't like Oliver Cromwell in Ireland) were pillaging the surrounding countryside, they disturbed a herd of goats. One injured he-goat, or puck, wandered into Killorglin, thus alerting the villagers to the approaching danger and allowing time to protect their

Don't know about you, but I'm pucked.

155

Smoked Kerry salmon

homes. Ever since, in honour of the goat's heroic, patriotic act, a puck is crowned King of Killorglin for the duration of the **Puck Fair** festival, which takes place each year beginning on 10 August. The fair includes lots of drinking, street theatre, eating, drinking, children's activities, circus acts, drinking, Irish dancing, live music, drinking, parades and drinking. It's the oldest fair in Ireland and it's not to be missed if you're lucky enough to be around.

The other thing that attracts visitors to the town, or more specifically the river, is the fishing. The River Laune is reputedly teeming with salmon and trout, just begging you to cast a line, snag their mouths with a barbed hook, yank them from the water, gut them, cook them and eat them. Ah, such is a salmon's lot!

About 10 km west of town along the N70 is the **Kerry Bog Village Museum**. It's a re-creation of a village from the nineteenth century, complete with whitewashed thatched cottages, authentic interiors and mannequin inhabitants.

Glenbeigh

Next up is the pretty village of Glenbeigh, nestling in the shadow of Curra Hill on a beautiful setting beside **Dingle Bay**. The village is a mecca for walking, golf, fishing, bird-watching, hang gliding, surfing, kayaking, or horse trekking. Whew! Exhausting. If you fancy a more relaxing stroll, **Rossbeigh Strand** is the place for you. The beach is just a short drive away, sits on its own little peninsula and is simply ginormous, with tremendous views across Dingle Bay. It is almost 3 km long and 200 m wide. There's also an interesting ruin of a nineteenth-century tower built as a navigation beacon, a replica of which stands in Glenbeigh village.

Cahirciveen

Continue westward along the N70, and the road is pretty scenic, especially when it swings towards the ocean. You'll pass beneath the pillars of the abandoned **Glenesk Viaduct**. It was part of the railway line that ran from Valentia Island to Farranfore Junction for nearly a hundred years before it closed in 1960. The journey was considered one of the most beautiful train journeys in the world at the time. Another 10 km brings you to Cahirciveen (also spelled Cahirsiveen).

It's a handsome town that's basically one very long street that seems to go on forever! Actually, the main bit that interests us and which has the accommodation, pubs, shops and restaurants is about a kilometre long. There's simply a gansey-load of good pubs, many serving fine food at reasonable prices, and lots of them with entertainment in the form of Irish music, singers and striptease artists. Perish the thought! The fine God-fearing folk of Cahirciveen have never had a sinful thought enter their heads!

Cahirciveen was the birthplace of Daniel O'Connell (see O'Connell Street). Dan the Man was a pacifist and didn't believe in blowing British soldiers' heads off but gained massive popular support via vast gatherings of hundreds of thousands of people. These 'Monster Meetings' scared the bejaysus out of the British government. Anyway, Dan is celebrated far and wide in Ireland.

Daniel 'The Liberator' O'Connell

In the centre of town stands **Daniel O'Connell Memorial Church**, which dates from the late nineteenth century and is Gothic in style. Also of interest in the church grounds is the grave of **Monsignor Hugh O'Flaherty**, a truly courageous priest who, like the famed Oscar Schindler, rescued thousands of Jews and Allied soldiers from the hands of the Gestapo during WWII. You could read all about his story and lots of other famed Irish people in *The Most Famous Irish People You've Never Heard Of*, which is a truly stupendous book that received rave reviews. Now, what was the author's name again?????

The **Old Constabulary Barracks** are to be found on the banks of the River Feartha, just before the bridge. The design looks sort of out of place and, according to local legend, the intention had been to build these barracks in India, but the plans got mixed up. But then, in the nineteenth century, the Brits rarely got anything right as regards Ireland! Ha ha. Sorry, British readers. Built in 1875, it is now an interesting **Heritage Centre and Museum**.

A short drive beyond the bridge will take you to the ruins of the seventeenth-century **Ballycarberry Castle**. And another short drive from there is **Cahergall Stone Fort**, which is an early Christian construction dating from around 600. A mere stroll away is the impressive **Leacanabuaile Stone Fort**, which is one of the best examples of an interior of a round stone fort in Ireland.

Valentia Island

Just past Cahirciveen along the N70 there's a sign for Valentia Island ferry. We're coming back via a bridge, so you won't need a return ticket. You'll land in the very charming little fishing village of **Knightstown**. There are some great pubs here, many with nautical-sounding names, not surprisingly, and an equally great bunch of restaurants, many with wonderful nautical menus, not surprisingly. The island itself is about 30 sq km and is rich in scenic views and interesting bits.

Here are the main sights, and probably in this order if travelling in an anti-clockwise direction. The cavernous **Slate Quarry and Grotto** towers thirty-five metres above you, appearing like a ginormous mouth in the face of the hillside. The quarry opened in 1816 and the high-quality slate was used on both the Paris Opera House and London's Houses of Parliament. The quarry closed in 1910 and in 1954 it was adapted as a religious grotto.

The Valentia Lighthouse sits just beyond the restored remnants of a Cromwellian fort on a small, isolated peninsula surrounded by scenery to swell the heart. The fort dates from the 1600s and the lighthouse, now automated, from the 1840s. A prehistoric **standing stone** three and a half metres high sits, or stands, in the middle of the fort.

A short drive away are the **Tetrapod Footprints**. These are a must. About three hundred and eighty million years ago, a four-legged vertebrate went for a stroll across some soft sand and left its footprints behind. These then hardened to rock, leaving us an invaluable record from the past. They're the most extensive of the four such tracks in the world, and are the oldest evidence of four-legged vertebrates moving over land.

Continue your anti-clockwise loop and watch for the privately owned **Geokaun Mountain and Fogher Cliffs**. You have to pay to visit, but it's cheap and worth your while. Calling it a mountain is a bit of a stretch – it's only two hundred and sixty six metres high – but the views from the top are stupendous. You can drive to the summit if you're feeling that lazy, and there's also a viewing point overlooking impressive cliffs.

Continue west and just as you reach the sea, the road forks and there's a small monument on your right. You probably don't know how much of a debt you owe to this place, as this was the birthplace of global communications. A **Trans-Atlantic cable** was laid across the Atlantic from this spot to Newfoundland, 3000 km away, the first such intercontinental connection. Completed in 1857, it was a vast undertaking. The cable was the catalyst for developing a global communications network.

Next up you'll see a bridge to the mainland on the right, and just before that **The Skellig Experience Visitor Centre**. It's only a fiver for adults to enter. The building itself is designed to reflect the structures on Skellig Michael and inside you'll find very interesting 3-D displays about life for the ancient monks, the island's birdlife and the Skellig lighthouses.

Portmagee

Farewell Valentia, hello Portmagee, which you'll encounter just as you cross the bridge. It's a tiny, but colourful little fishing village – basically a single street overlooking the sea.

And yet in recent years Portmagee has had international stardom thrust upon it! Why? Basically because the crew and cast filming the latest *Star Wars* movies liked to use the village's pubs to chill out! Pictures were sent around the globe at light speed of Luke Skywalker, aka Mark Hamill, pulling a pint of Guinness and tucking heartily into bags of Tayto Crisps (the best potato snack in the universe, by the way!) and Rey, aka Daisy Ridley, joining in during a traditional Irish music session, along with the rest of the *Star*

So are you working on this movie as well?

Wars gang enjoying a wrap party in **The Bridge Bar** late into the night. **The Fisherman's Bar** was also a favourite of the intergalactic visitors.

A very short drive from the village are the **Kerry Cliffs**, which are worth the small entry fee.

Ballinskelligs

Obviously this village has close links with Skellig Michael (the clue is in the name!) but it isn't really a village as such, more a collection of houses and a couple of pubs and cafés spread out along a country road. It has a marvellous **golden beach** upon which sits the ruin of a medieval castle.

Ballinskelligs is also in the centre of Kerry's **International Dark Sky Reserve**. The what, you ask? It means that on clear nights, the sky in this part of Europe is stunning in its clarity thanks to the lack of light or particle pollution, with a great many astronomical sights visible to the naked eye. It is one of only three Gold Tier Reserves on the planet. All you need is a clear sky. In your dreams, pal!

Waterville

Waterville is a lovely village in a beautiful setting, nestling between the gorgeous Lough Currane and the Atlantic. It offers multiple choices of good accommodation, pubs and restaurants.

In terms of history and heritage, here's some stuff to watch out for. Right along the waterfront road you'll see a **statue of Charlie Chaplin**, of all folk. You see, the movie legend came here on holidays in 1959 and loved the place so much that he and his family came back every year for much of the rest of his life.

Just along from Charlie is a statue of another legend, this time a local one. **Mick O'Dwyer** actually unveiled the statue of himself in 2012 – you might even catch a glimpse of the man wandering by his own statue! Mick distinguished himself during a long career as a Gaelic Football player and manager, winning four All-Ireland medals for County Kerry,

To be fair, he never said much in his movies either.

and then as a manager directing his young Kerry charges in winning an astounding eight All-Ireland titles. You really have to be Irish to appreciate the size of this achievement.

If you're a golfy type, you may be interested to know that **Waterville Golf Links** is rated among the top twenty links courses in the world. Many of the world's top golfers have played here at some point.

A short drive from town you'll see a sign for the impressive **Loher Stone Fort**, which dates from the eighth/ninth century and was built as a defended farmstead, and when the chieftain wasn't battling off Vikings, he could enjoy fab views. On top of all that, my brother lives a stone's throw away.

Caherdaniel

You get an idea of Caherdaniel's size from the fact that it contains only two pubs! Small as it is, it is overflowing with Irish history. The nearby **Derrynane House** was the home of

Daniel O'Connell. Mahatma Gandhi and Martin Luther King both said that O'Connell was among their greatest sources of inspiration. British PM Gladstone said he was 'the greatest popular leader the world has ever seen.' Anyway, you can learn a lot more about his life and times at the historic house, which nestles in the delightful Derrynane **National Historic Park,** some three hundred acres of beautifully laid-out gardens and walkways. A visit is a must.

If you've got kids with you, you have our sympathies. But on a positive note, you may take solace from the fact that within the grounds of Derrynane House you'll find **Irish Fairy Trails**, a charming little woodland area in which your sweet darlings will discover a collection of fairy homes to delight their little hearts.

Just to the east of the village is **O'Carroll's Cove**, a lovely sheltered little beach with a pub and seafood restaurant, and views to treasure as you dig into your fresh local prawns served on brown Irish soda bread. Mmmmm...

Sneem

What else can you say but that Sneem is bewitching? It consists of two little triangular greens separated by a bridge across the Sneem River. The houses are a feast of colours, the pubs and restaurants are massive, deadly and savage (all slang for 'fantastic'). The riverside setting is gorgeous and there are lots of interesting bits to explore. What more could you want?

Take a wander around. Pause on the **bridge** and look west. The view has been captured in oils many a time.

There are lots of sculptures you should look out for. In fact, it's probably safe to say that Sneem has more sculptures and monuments per capita than anywhere else in Ireland. In **South Square** there's a memorial to ex-**President of Ireland, Cearbhall Ó Dálaigh** who is buried here. Unfortunately his memorial resembles part of the fuselage of a crashed jumbo jet. Then there's a titan of Sneem lore in **Steve 'Crusher' Casey**. It's a life-size bronze sculpture of this muscled giant who was nine times Heavyweight World Wrestling Champion.

Next to St Michael's Catholic Church is an unusual bronze depiction of Christ, which was created by Irish-Singaporean sculptor, Brother Joseph McNally. Not the usual tormented Christ to make you feel guilty for being a wojus sinner, the **Risen Christ** is an elegant bronze figure flowing up from the earth.

Go down the other side of the church and you're on **The Way of the Fairies**, which is part of the **Sculpture Park**. It's a collection of stone structures also known as **The Pyramids**, inspired by the ancient monks' beehive huts. You'll also find a statue of the **Goddess Isis**. What in the name of Jaysus is a pagan goddess doing right beside a Catholic church in holy, Christian Ireland? Well, apparently the Egyptian ambassador so enjoyed his sojourns to the village that he donated it as a gift from the people of Egypt. Ye gods!

The mighty Pyramids of Sneem

In **North Square** you'll see a monument to former French **President Charles de Gaulle**. You see, the legendary Frenchman legged it to Sneem immediately after resigning in 1969, in search of peace and tranquillity. Of Sneem he said: 'At this grave moment of my long life, I found here what I sought, to be face to face with myself, Ireland gave me that, in the most delicate, the most friendly way.' Nous vous aimons, Charles!

Just behind this is the **Tree of Light** – a metal yoke that reflects the sunlight on the three days of the year there is some. It was a gift from the people of Israel to the village for the assistance that President Ó Dálaigh gave to the Jewish community in Ireland.

Kenmare

And so we come to Kenmare, a lovely little town designed around a triangle of three streets with a nice triangular green at their apex. Like Sneem, it's a colourful place with myriad brightly painted homes, shops, pubs and restaurants. And most of those 'refreshment retreats' are feckin' massive.

The town and surrounding area have enough activities to leave your body banjaxed and ready for chilling. There's a gansey-load of walks, a golf course, cycling routes, kayaking, horse riding and a bunch of other activities for the so-inclined. If you are one of the lazy not-so-inclined, you might find comfort in the more relaxing pursuit of things historical. Failing that, you can just go to the pub, a worthy pursuit in itself, especially as you're on holiday and nobody's going to tell you off.

Henry Street and **Main Street** are where you'll find most of the shops, pubs and restaurants. A walk around town with your nearest and dearest will take you less than five minutes, unless your partner decides to either have a pint in every pub, or buy something in every shop, in which case it will take you five hours.

At the northwestern corner of the green you'll see the narrow Market Street. A five-minute walk up here will take you to **Kenmare Stone Circle**. It's one of the largest stone circles in southwest Ireland, measuring almost eighteen metres across, and it dates from 2000–500 BC. These fascinating ancient monuments are believed to be for ritual burial and ceremonial purposes. The Kenmare circle is composed of fifteen large boulders with an impressive dolmen in the centre, under which presumably lies the poor eejit that croaked it.

Returning to the green, on the left is the short Bridge Street, which gives pedestrian access to the fourteenth-century **Cromwell's Bridge**, erected by Augustinian monks. Spanning the small Finnihy River, it has an unusual inverted U-shape design. Looking at it, you'd imagine it would have been easier to just wade across rather than clamber awkwardly over the top!

A short dander from the bridge is **Our Lady's Well**, a tranquil little grotto to the Blessed Virgin, and its waters are said to have curative powers for the faithful. Perhaps it

might work on your hangover? You never know.

If you fancy a brief excursion, you could do worse than spend a couple of enjoyable hours exploring **Bonane Heritage Park**, which is 5 km south of the town along the N71. This is an area in which a treasure trove of ancient archaeology was recently discovered. There are standing stones, a ringfort, a stone circle and a bunch of other bits from time immemorial. There's also the ruin of an abandoned 'famine cottage' and a Fairy Walk with fairy houses to amuse the little darlings. There's a small entry fee.

Moll's Gap and beyond...

We're on the last leg of our circuit, and you'll probably agree that the Ring's legs are even more beautiful than Katy Perry's. But the best is yet to come!

Head north towards **Moll's Gap** on the N71 – it's about 10km, and the drive is very pretty, especially as it begins to climb. Moll's Gap, which is named after **Moll Kissane** who ran a shebeen (illicit pub) during the construction of the original road in the early nineteenth century, selling home-made poitín to the workers, making her a very popular lady. Poitín, in case you've forgotten, is an illicit spirit that, if consumed to excess, will result in a hangover that will deprive you of your will to live. Anyway, there's a shop and café there and some tremendous views.

Continue on the N71 towards Killarney. Suffice it to say that the 20km descent is one of the most beautiful drives you will ever take in your life. *Really*. It's a winding route through green, rugged mountains, loughs and woodlands with panoramas to lift the heart. If you're lucky, you'll see it when the purple heather and bright yellow furze bushes are ablaze with colour in the summer. Take your time – stop at every chance you get and breathe in the scenery and fresh mountain air and hope that your camera doesn't run out of memory space.

And so we're back to Killarney, at journey's end. Now, where's the nearest pub?

The Japanese Gardens at the Irish National Stud

29. Irish National Stud and Gardens

Besides hospitality, scenery, pubs, food, music, literature, hurling and U2, Ireland is also famed for its horses. The National Stud is a magnet for horsey folk from all over the world, not least Queen Elizabeth II, who visited in 2011, or the Aga Khan, who has a long association with the place. But don't worry if you don't know a horse's head from its arse, because this place should still be on your must-do list, as besides things equestrian, you'll also find the wonderful Japanese Gardens, which are considered the finest of their kind in Europe and are actually why the majority of people visit.

But first the horsey stuff. Ireland's history with our big four-legged friends goes back to about 2000 BC, so we've

had plenty of time to get it right. And that we did, as we've been breeding champion after champion racehorses for, eh, donkey's years. True horse-racing fans will marvel at the sight of the now-retired Beef Or Salmon, Hardy Eustace, Hurricane Fly, Kicking King and Rite Of Passage grazing serenely in their paddock, appropriately dubbed the **Living Legends** enclosure. To put this in perspective, this is like a music fan discovering Frank Sinatra, Paul McCartney, Louis Armstrong and Adele having a pint together in a pub. **The Horse Museum** also provides a fascinating look at Ireland's long association with the great beast, with lots of artefacts and memorabilia. And the centrepiece is the skeleton of **Arkle**, regarded as the greatest steeplechaser in the history of the planet. We even invented that term 'steeplechase', y'know? Back in 1752, Cornelius O'Callaghan and Edmund Blake had a bet on a race between the steeples in two towns, thus giving the world 'steeplechase'.

But to be honest, the majority of visitors are here for the **Japanese Gardens**, and the more recent **St Fiachra's Garden**. The original gardens were the vision of a wealthy Scottish brewer called William Hall Walker, and in 1906, he hired the Japanese master horticulturist Tassa Eida and his son Minoru to design them. The stunning gardens take you on a journey through 'The Life of Man' (and one has to assume, Woman, as well). Each section is representative of a different stage of existence: oblivion, birth, childhood, learning, marriage, screaming rows and divorce, death and eternity. OK, we made up the bit about the screaming rows. The journey is a magical odyssey through colourful exotic plants, across waterfalls, stepping-stones and bridges, and past Oriental structures and shrines.

St Fiachra's Garden was laid out in 1999, in honour of the patron saint of gardeners, and reflects the ancient monastic life lived amid the Irish landscape. It's also got a nice sculpture of the holy guy, sitting reflecting on the edge of a pond.

Horses or horticulture? Take your pick. As they say at the National Stud, people come for the gardens but stay for the horses.

St Mary's Cathedral, Kilkenny city

30. Kilkenny City

Kilkenny is one of Ireland's oldest and most beautiful cities and it was even the capital of Ireland for a while until that murdering scumbag Cromwell invaded! It's still got something of a medieval feel, although luckily they don't have public floggings, unless, that is, you say anything to disrespect their hurling team.

No, wait - I said it was the footballers that are rubbish!

The historic centre of the small city sits between the fab Kilkenny Castle to the south and the lovely St Canice's Cathedral to the north. In between is a medieval grid of narrow streets where some of the ancient structures nestle beside their more modern counterparts. You might find yourself having a pint in a pub that was established in the thirteenth century, although they've hopefully moved beyond serving mead with pig's brains. The city also benefits from its setting on the beautiful **River Nore**.

The **Medieval Mile** is a recommended route that takes in many of the sights. It basically starts at **Kilkenny Castle**, which dates from the twelfth century and is in great nick considering it's eight hundred years old. It's a huge castle with towers and turrets and all that medieval stuff. It has a very colourful history, and a gorgeous riverside setting and wonderful gardens. There's a charge for tours but the park and gardens are free.

Just across the road from the castle sits the **National Craft Gallery** and, if you head up **The Parade**, you'll come to **High Street**, which has an eclectic mix of shops, cafés, pubs and nice old buildings. Watch for a turn on the right into St Mary's Lane, taking you to **St Mary's Medieval Mile Museum**, which gives a great modern take on history, and is set in a splendidly restored medieval church.

High Street becomes **Parliament Street**, which leads to **St Canice's Cathedral and Round Tower**. The site was founded in the sixth century, the Cathedral is a Gothic architectural gem and you also have the opportunity of climbing the Round Tower – there are only two in Ireland where you can do this, so seize the day! In nearby Abbey Street you can see the fourteenth-century **Black Abbey**, a restored Catholic

Great - they finally let us in and there's nothing to steal

St. Canice's Cathedral and Round Tower

church with a magnificent stained-glass window.

Last but not least, the mile route takes you back towards the castle along **St Kieran's Street** and one of the oldest pubs in Ireland, which is a great place to end up. It's called **Kyteler's** after Dame Alice Kyteler, who was accused of murdering three of her husbands and of sorcery, was then tried for witchcraft in Ireland's first ever such trial, but escaped and fled to England. So naturally they burned her poor maid, Petronella, instead. There's something to reflect upon as you savour a pint in Kyteler's. Ah you can't beat a bit of medieval brutality!

Glencar Waterfall, County Leitrim

31. Leitrim's Loughs and Glencar Waterfall

County Leitrim is famed in Ireland for three things. It has hapes and hapes (that's 'heaps' in a sort-of Leitrim accent) of loughs, it has the lowest population of any county in Ireland so there's loads of space for all those loughs, and they are one of the few teams that have never won a football or hurling All-Ireland Championship! But at least they can comfort themselves with all the great fishing.

There are roughly two hundred loughs in Leitrim and the place is a mecca for anglers from far and wide. But if sitting for hours waiting for an unfortunate fish to have its jaws torn open by a hook isn't your idea of great craic, not to worry, there's plenty of other stuff to see. Take one of the scenic drives such as that along the shores of **Glenade Lough, Lough Melvin, Lough Allen** or **Lough Gill** and you'll see what we're talking about. Leitrim also boasts a whole range of walking/hiking, nature and riverside trails, and given that the county has Ireland's lowest population density at twenty people per square kilometre, you're guaranteed peace and quiet.

THE SEA
LOVELY
LEITRIM
LOUGH MELVIN.
GLENCAR LOUGH
GLENADE LAKE
LOUGH McNEAN
VERY QUIET.
NOBODY ABOUT
LOUGH GILL
LOUGH ALLEN
SILENCE
LOUGH SCUR
GARADICE LAKE
PEACE + QUIET.
LOUGH RYNN
LOUGH BOFIN

And one of the nicest drives of all is the short drive along **Glencar Lough**, which nestles amid steep-sided hills from which tumbles a river that has sculpted a movie-set-like location into the hillside, in the form of **Glencar Waterfall**. It's sixteen metres high and the water seems to pour from amid the overhanging vegetation into a pool surrounded by a horseshoe-shaped rock wall. It's like something out of a Yeats poem. Come to think of it, it *is* out of a Yeats poem:

> Where the wandering water gushes
> From the hills above Glen-Car,
> In pools among the rushes
> That scarce could bathe a star,
> We seek for slumbering trout
> And whispering in their ears
> Give them unquiet dreams;
> Leaning softly out
> From ferns that drop their tears
> Over the young streams.
>
> From 'The Stolen Child' by WB Yeats

And if it's good enough for WB Yeats, it's certainly good enough for the likes of you!

Thatched cottage, Adare, County Limerick

32. Adare

This is arguably the prettiest village in Ireland, although the locals will tell you there's no argument. It's always a good sign when a place is really popular for getting hitched – love-struck young couples want to cling desperately to

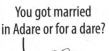
You got married in Adare or for a dare?

sweet memories of a beautiful setting for their nuptials when years later they're yelling at each other while trying to dress a bunch of snotty-nosed kids on a wet Tuesday in November. So it can be tricky some-times to get accommo-dation here, as all the rooms are taken up with girls in fancy wedding dresses and fellas look-ing uncomfortable in stiff suits, especially at weekends, so book well in advance if you'd like to stay awhile.

It's not a huge place, it probably hovers somewhere between the definitions for 'village' and 'town', but despite its size, it packs a load of stuff in in terms of historic sites, gorgeous houses, great pubs and restaurants and general ambience. And it's even got a world-class golf course.

Bits to see

For a whirlwind tour of the historic sites, start on the eastern end, approaching the village along the main N21. As you cross the bridge over the **River Maigue** you'll see the impressive ruin of a twelfth-century castle sitting beside the river on your left. This is **Desmond Castle**, named after the powerful family of lords who last owned the place in the medieval period. You can't visit it on your own, which is a shame, but regular tours are organised through the Heritage Centre.

Nearby is another imposing ruin, that of the **Franciscan Friary**, which dates from 1464. Although it's slap bang in the middle of Adare Manor golf course, you can access it – just watch for low-flying balls from lousy golfers.

On the right just over the bridge is the entrance to the **Augustinian Friary**. Although it dates from the fourteenth century it's perfectly preserved thanks to having been converted into a Church of Ireland church.

Next up is the entrance to **Adare Manor Hotel** on the left. It's a neo-Gothic masterpiece on magnificent grounds. It was built by the local toffs in the mid-nineteenth century. If you can't afford to stay, drop in for a pint or some afternoon tea!

As you enter the main street of the town, you'll see a collection of adorable **thatched cottages** on the left. They were built as part of the Adare Manor Estate in the 1820s. They serve mostly as charming tearooms, craft shops, etc.

now, and you'll definitely be posting pics of yourself here on your Facebook page.

Straight across the road on your right is the **Trinitarian Abbey**, originally founded in the thirteenth century, but restored in the nineteenth. It's a lovely old building and currently serves as the Catholic parish church, so don't go in snapping pictures if mass is on!

There's a pleasant little park on the left where you can rest your feet now, or else you can nip across the road to the **Heritage Centre** for more insights into the village. Or alternatively you can continue on through the town and explore the nice collection of pretty restaurants and pubs down the western end, which sounds like a plan to us...

Out of the frying pan
and into the friary?

King John's Castle on the banks of the Shannon, Limerick

33. King John's Castle

It probably scared the bejaysus out of potential attackers approaching along the River Shannon or from across the bridge to the east, because even today, King John's Castle presents a forbidding face to the world, so you can imagine how it must have looked eight hundred years ago. It's without doubt one of the best-preserved Norman castles in Europe.

The history bit

King John of England built it at the start of the thirteenth century, although it's doubtful he ever lifted a trowel of mortar. His brother, Henry II, was actually the first English king to stick his nose into Irish affairs, and countless millions of unwelcome Brit noses would continue to stick around for the next eight hundred years. The castle was built to defend Limerick against rebelling Gaelic chieftains.

The thick walls and imposing towers did their job well until 1641, when a bit of Irish ingenuity got the better of them. When it was occupied by Protestants during the Irish Rebellion of 1641, Irish Confederate forces led by Garret Barry began a siege. Unfortunately Barry had no siege artillery so couldn't send any cannonballs over the walls to splatter his enemies into mush. So instead of going over, he went under. He had his troops dig away at the foundations until part of the wall was about to collapse, at which point the inhabitants surrendered.

So much for the intruder alarm.

Medieval makeover

But you'll get much more detail on all the disembowelling, throat-cutting, decapitating, etc. that people liked to do back then when you visit the castle. And it's recently reopened after a major face-lift that cost more money than Donald Trump's hair transplant, and that's a lot. It's thirteenth century meets twenty-first century, with all sorts of gleaming 3-D exhibition wizardry, computer animations, ghostly historical figures, models of Limerick, costumed guides and lots of other interesting stuff. Incidentally, the best place to take snaps of the castle is from Clancy's Strand Road – just go across the bridge and turn left. It's especially impressive at night when it's illuminated.

Looking downriver from the bridge at Drumsna, County Leitrim

34. The River Shannon

One could write tome upon tome about the River Shannon given its length, the diversity of landscape through which it flows, its huge importance in Irish history, its sporting and recreational aspects and loads of other stuff, but we've only got a page or two to fill you in, so we'll do our best.

Here are the basics. It's the longest river in Ireland or Britain at 360 km, and drains an area of about 17,000 sq km, or one-fifth of Ireland. That length doesn't include the Shannon Estuary where the river meets the Atlantic, and that's over

100 km long itself and about 12 km wide at its mouth. It flows through eleven counties and three major loughs and a bunch of smaller ones. Is that enough watery facts for ye?

The source of the Shannon

Guess what the best way to experience the River Shannon is? Yes, by God, you're smart. By train. No, we're kidding. By boat, of course. **Cruising the Shannon** is a hugely popular activity with visitors and Irish people alike. That's especially true as it doesn't matter if you can tell a gunwale from a transom from a coxswain to hire one out – all instruction is provided by the multiplicity of boat-hire companies along the route. It's also relatively cheap considering the boat becomes your lodging and your means of travel. And when you hit a calm, unspoilt part of the landscape far from the madding crowds, traffic and roads, you'll chill like never before. Especially if the weather is freezing.

There are heaps of pretty towns to visit along the river and lots of places of historic or scenic interest, like **Athlone Castle**, **Clonmacnoise Monastic site**, **Lough Key Park**, **Arigna Mines** and **Holy Island** in **Lough Derg**, as well as a gazillion more. So leave your land legs behind, because a Shannon cruise will really float your boat.

Carlingford Castle, County Louth

35. Carlingford and Cooley Peninsula

Carlingford is a fine little village in a glorious setting with a nice collection of medieval sites that reflect its long history. In its time it has been invaded, sacked, burned to the ground, rebuilt and invaded again, which is hard to believe when you see how feckin' peaceful the place is. There's still the odd invasion, but don't worry, they're just invasions of tourists, anglers, hillwalkers or people eager to savour its nice pubs and restaurants.

Carlingford sits between Slieve Foy to the west and the gorgeous Carlingford Lough to the east and north, and across the lough rise the impressive peaks of the Mourne Mountains in County Down. The town and peninsula have an eclectic selection of great pubs and restaurants, and its seaside setting guarantees you're going to find some great, fresh seafood here.

An invading force of tourists is approaching Sire. Hundreds of them.

The history bit

The natural harbour was a tempting sight to bloodthirsty Vikings, who invaded in the ninth century and gave the place its name – the Fjord of Carlinn. Medieval times gave it a lasting heritage of impressive buildings, now in ruins,

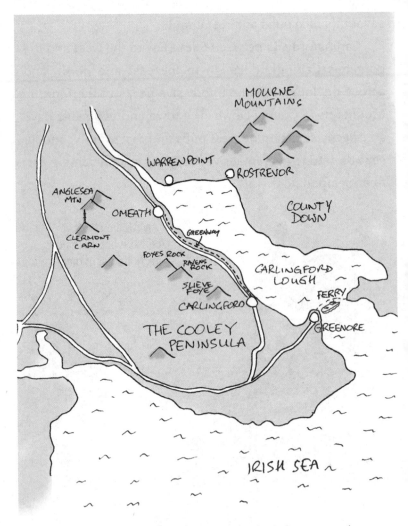

including **King John's Castle**, which rises from a rocky out-crop by the shore. **Taaffe's Castle**, the **Thosel** or town gate, the **Mint** and the **Dominican Friary** are just a stroll from the village centre, so you don't even have to strain your leg muscles to experience a whole heap of history.

194

Way to go!

The Cooley Peninsula is also home to the **Cooley Mountains**, which overlook the lough and the Irish Sea, so there are scenic drives aplenty, and like the local cuisine, it's scenery to make your mouth water. The drive along the lough towards **Omeath** to the north is splendiferous, but you might also venture along some of the minor roads in the Cooley Mountains – you can actually drive to the summit of **Clermont Carn** thanks to the presence of a communications mast. The mountain is over five hundred metres high and has great views of the surrounding landscape.

Carlingford and the Peninsula are naturally a magnet for walkers. Those who prefer a gentle stroll might like the relative ease of the **Carlingford Greenway** that runs along the shore towards Omeath. Others who fancy themselves as more energetic types can work up a sweat and a thirst by venturing into the many hillwalking routes in the mountains. The Lough also makes the area very popular with watersporty types, anglers and boaters. Oh, and you'll even have an opportunity to try your hand at foot golf!

Bridge on the Great Western Greenway, County Mayo

36. The Great Western Greenway

Time to abandon the car, folks, because the Greenway is all about leg power. This cycling or walking route steers clear of roads and allows you to truly appreciate the Mayo countryside, the tranquillity and the fresh Irish air, and as they say in the west, it's only massive.

The 19.37 train from Westport to Achill has been cancelled.

The Greenway is almost 45 km long, hugging the coast of Clew Bay and taking in the lovely towns of Westport, Newport and Mulranny before finishing on the achingly beautiful Achill Island. Up until 1937, trains thundered along the route but the long-abandoned line has now been cleverly adapted for use by the more leisurely traveller, the work having been completed in 2011. There are no real hills to climb and no fences to traverse, so it's a relatively easy trek even for the laziest among us.

It begins/ends in Westport or Achill, but a small tip – the prevailing winds in Ireland tend to be south to north, so as usual we'll always look for the easiest option and start in **Westport**, and we'll refer you to the separate entry for that very lovely town.

The first section of the Greenway will take you to New-port, a distance of 11 km. That's about three hours' easy walking, It will take you across lush green pastures and through pleasant woodland, and even though the trail tends to run alongside a road for a good part of its length, it doesn't detract from the enjoyment of the countryside.

Newport is a pleasant little town on the Newport River, overlooked by St Patrick's Church perched on a hill, and with a fine old rail viaduct. Its greatest claim to fame is that it is the ancestral home of Princess Grace of Monaco, formerly Grace Kelly. How's that for posh? The route from here to Mulranny is the longest section, at 18 km. Allow six hours if you're walking. Although it initially hugs the road, after a few kilometres the Greenway and road go their separate ways, taking you through unspoiled open countryside, across old bridges and through tranquil woodland.

Although your legs might be banjaxed, your eyes will feel totally enlivened by the view that greets them on arrival in the pretty village of **Mulranny**, which looks out over the expanse of Clew Bay towards the rising hills to the south. And the final part of your journey is undoubtedly the most scenic. You can relish 13 km (three hours' walking) of spectacular mountains, loughs, rivers and more pic ops than your smartphone memory can handle.

Achill Island, your final destination, is linked to the mainland by a short bridge. And though the Greenway ends here, sure the scenery is only beginning. Achill is steeped in history and beauty. It's a large island with 150 sq km of soaring hills, towering sea cliffs, golden beaches, and sea and landscapes you'll want to grab and take home with you!

And when you've done all that, why not head back the way you came?

Ashford Castle, Cong, County Mayo

37. Cong

Mary Kate Danaher: It's a bold one you are! Who gave you leave to be kissin' me?

Thornton: So you can talk!

Mary Kate Danaher: Yes I can, I will and I do! And it's more than talk you'll be getting if you step a step closer to me!

You might recognise that little scene from the classic 1950s movie, *The Quiet Man*, starring John Wayne and Maureen O'Hara. And what's it got to do with the gorgeous little village of Cong? Well, the whole movie was shot in and around here and in nearby Ashford Castle, and the village has been making dosh from that fact ever since. Having said that, even without *The Quiet Man* connection, it's got loads of stuff to see.

Fit for a king

The village sits on the **Cong River** and its most famous historical landmark is **Cong Abbey**, a nineteenth-century ruin that's slap bang in the middle of the village and is regarded as a masterpiece of medieval architecture. It is also renowned as the place where Ireland's last High King, Rory O'Connor, spent his final years before kicking the bucket in 1198, no doubt glad of a bit of peace and quiet after all the years of slicing up his enemies. In the grounds you'll see a little architectural gem in the fifteenth-century **Monk's Fishing House**, a clever little structure built over the river, so that when the fish swam through a gap underneath, the monks could nab them easily. A ten-minute walk to the west, via a trail from the village, you'll find **Pigeon Hole Cave**. The small cavern (magical too, according to Irish mythology anyway) lies at the foot of a series of stone steps that descend through moss-covered walls of stone.

Wayne's World...

As regards *The Quiet Man*, there is a selection of yokes to see, not least of which is the terrific bronze statue of **John Wayne carrying Maureen O'Hara** in his arms, which captures the pair and the movie scene perfectly. There's also **Pat Cohan's Bar**, which featured in a number of scenes. It's just been refurbished in a simple style that manages to retain the character of the 1950s era, and the food here is reputedly fit for a movie star. Then there's **The Quiet Man**

Museum, located in a sweet thatched cottage and replicating the Danahers' home in the movie. And there are loads of other movie references and locations about the village.

Perhaps the biggest movie location of all is that of **Ashford Castle** about a kilometre from the village, and in whose grounds a whole bunch of scenes were shot. *The Quiet Man* aside, the Castle, which is now a luxury hotel, is a star worthy of any movie. It's a magnificent, fairytale-like building that has been in the making for centuries. Among former guests it can number Oscar Wilde, King George V, John Lennon, George Harrison, President Ronald Reagan, Brad Pitt, Robin Williams, Pierce Brosnan, who had his wedding here, and Rory McIlroy, who also tied the knot in the Castle. And a whole bunch of others. Even if you can't afford a room, go in and have a gawk anyway and imagine what it must be like to be rich!

St Patrick statue and Croagh Patrick, Westport, County Mayo

38. Westport and Croagh Patrick

In 2012, *The Irish Times* ran a competition called 'The Best Places to Live in Ireland', and guess where won? No, it wasn't 'Above a pub'. It was Westport, of course! It's not surprising, as Wesport is a sweet spot indeed. The River Carrowbeg runs through the leafy heart of town, its well-kept streets are a collection of colourful and historic buildings, and not too far away the old Westport Quay area gazes across towards the fabled Croagh Patrick.

Bits to see and a bit of history

Take a stroll along **The Mall**, the tree-lined riverside that was laid out in 1800 and still looks as good today. At the lower bridge you'll see the fine, nineteenth-century neo-Gothic **Holy Trinity Church** a little along to your right. To your left is James Street, which leads you up to **The Octagon**, the town's focal point. There's a sizeable collection of great pubs here, which is always a good sign. The central column and statue have an interesting history. The column was originally topped by a statue of George Glendenning, a rich land agent, who was a much-despised figure in Ireland, especially during the Great Famine. During the Irish Civil War, troops used the statue for target practice and managed to decapitate old George. Eventually he was replaced, somewhat more appropriately, by **St Patrick**.

If you're done with the pubs in the Octagon, turn left up

Shop Street, and perhaps do a little leisurely shopping, and when you reach the clock tower turn left again towards The Mall along Bridge Street, which is jammers with nice restaurants, coffee shops, pubs and an eclectic mix of shops.

When you're done, take a wander out to **Westport Quay**, which is about 2 km away and is a charming area of restored warehouses, some of which now serve as restaurants, pubs or hotels. The quay itself is 500 metres long and during the nineteenth century witnessed heart-

breaking scenes of families departing forever for the New World. Nowadays it's a pleasant spot for a stroll and has great views of Croagh Patrick.

Just at the start of the quay you'll see a small road leading to **Westport House**. This is a fab, three-century-old stately home, and now a visitor attraction. You can visit thirty magnificent rooms and see how the local toffs used to lord it over the smelly peasants! You can also visit the beautiful estate and there's even a pirate adventure yoke for the kids.

Croagh Patrick mountain, about 5 km from town, is so named because St Patrick reputedly fasted for forty days on the mountain in 441. It's an iconic mountain, quartz-topped, giving it a striking appearance. It's a place of pilgrimage and on the last Sunday of each July thousands of the faithful climb its steep, very rocky track to the summit (seven hundred and forty six metres). Go on! Have a crack! It can only kill you! Besides, some of the people who make the pilgrimage are in their seventies and others do it barefoot! The views from the summit are certainly heavenly, taking in the sweep of Clew Bay, which reputedly has 'an island for every day of the year'.

While you're there, don't miss the **National Famine Monument** near the foot of the mountain. It's a striking sculpture by John Behan, depicting a ship, part of which is composed of the skeletal figures of the starving or those fleeing on the countless 'coffin ships'.

The entrance to Newgrange, County Meath

39. Newgrange

Six hundred years before some ancient Egyptian head-the-ball built a pyramid, a similar amount of time before the Brits thought up Stonehenge, and nearly three thousand years before the Romans began conquering the world, the Irish built Newgrange. Which just goes to prove what a race of geniuses we are.

Newgrange is one of the most important megalithic structures in Europe, it's the oldest astronomical observatory in the world and it's a **UNESCO World Heritage Site**.

It takes the form of an eighty-metre wide, grassy, circular mound, partly enclosed by a wall of white quartz A narrow passage extends almost twenty metres towards the centre, at the end of which are three small inner chambers.

I got the idea when I was on holidays in Ireland

Actually Newgrange is only one part of the UNESCO site and there are two other parts nearby called **Knowth** and **Dowth**.

You can only visit Newgrange and Knowth via the **Brú na Bóinne Visitor Centre** and take a guided tour. So let's make tracks and step back into the mysterious world of Neolithic Ireland.

Let there be light

Just before dawn on the morning of 21 December 1967 (the winter solstice), the renowned Irish archaeologist **Michael J O'Kelly** was excavating away in the inner chamber at Newgrange when a startling thing happened. As the sun rose above the horizon, the chamber was suddenly flooded with light, like something out of an Indiana Jones movie. O'Kelly realised that the ancients had aligned the passage precisely to catch the sun at dawn on the shortest day of the year. There are hundreds of passage tombs in Ireland, Scotland and Wales, but none are as precisely designed as Newgrange.

Among the bits discovered at Newgrange are cremated human bones, stone marbles, four pendants, a highly polished granite container and lid, decorated beads, stone axe heads, flint flakes, a bone chisel, and two gold Roman coins, which is odd as the Romans never got around to conquering Ireland. But they did send a few scouting missions in the fourth century, then probably saw the weather and thought 'f*** this! They can keep the place!'

Despite the fact that experts have been poking about the place, taking measurements, digging up stuff and so on for centuries, the purpose of Newgrange is still shrouded in mystery. It may have been a temple to sun-worshippers. Or to a religion that venerated the dead. Or an astronomical calendar of sorts. Or It may also have been a fancy burial place for important Neolithic big shots.

As you approach the entrance, you'll see a row of **standing stones** partially encircling the building. There are twelve of these remaining although there were thirty-even originally. The white, quartz wall covering the front side of the mound is a reconstruction – the stones were scattered about in the surrounding field having collapsed down the decades.

Huge kerbstones, many of which are covered in megalithic

The neolithic sun-worshippers of Newgrange

art, ring the entire mound. The ginormous **Entrance Stone** is the best decorated and is regarded as a masterpiece of European Neolithic art. It may have acted as a threshold between this world and the world of the dead. Creepy.

Look up above the entrance and you'll see the **roofbox** – that's the big slab propped across two other slabs. That's there for a very important reason, but we'll get to that.

Beyond the entrance stone you're into the **passage**, and hopefully you haven't got claustrophobia as it's not exactly roomy. Many of these were decorated by the ancients and a few were decorated by gobshite graffiti artists.

The end of the passage opens into a larger **inner chamber** with alcoves on three sides. Within each alcove sits a basin stone and it was into these that the Neolithics put your bones after you'd croaked it. The roof is so well designed that it has kept out the water for five millennia, which is more than can be said for the gouger who repaired my roof.

It's in here where the magic happens. And if you happen

to be there sometime other than on the winter solstice, or if it's bucketing rain outside and there's no sign of the sun, no problemo, Your tour guide will turn off the lights and flick a switch, simulating the sun as it appears on the shortest day of the year, the light pouring through the roofbox, spilling down the passage and flooding the inner chamber. Those Irish Neolithics sure were an illuminated bunch in every sense.

Knowth and Dowth

Although these might sound like cute robots from *Star Wars*, they are in fact Newgrange's sister sites and they're both less than 2 km away.

Knowth is in many ways even more interesting than Newgrange. For starters, it looks like the set of a Hobbit village from *Lord of the Rings*. It takes the form of a huge grassy mound 67 metres across and 12 high, surrounded by 17 smaller mounds. Knowth is the largest passage tomb in the complex and contains two passages, one leading to a chamber similar to that at Newgrange. But get this, Knowth is said to contain more than a third of all known examples of megalithic art in Western Europe. Unfortunately, for archaeological reasons you aren't allowed enter the passage at Knowth, but you can look into it.

There are no tours to Dowth unfortunately and it's the least well-preserved of the three sites. In fact, it looks a bit neglected at times. You can drive there and simply walk up to it along a short path. The mound is over 80 metres wide and 15 high and contains two short passages leading to chambers. One of the passages is also aligned precisely to capture the sun's rays during the winter solstice. But unless you're an important visiting archaeologist, you can't access the interior. Aww. Still, the good thing is that because it's so undeveloped as an attraction, on some days you could have the place to yourself.

Brú na Bóinne Visitor Centre

The name literally means 'Palace of the Boyne' and refers to the entire area encompassing the three principal mounds. The Visitor Centre contains all sorts of colourful interactive displays and exhibits, including a partial full-scale replica of the chamber at Newgrange. The Centre is spacious, modern and well-designed and has a restaurant and gift shop, and of course, toilets – facilities at the actual sites are limited, i.e. you'll have to go in the bushes.

A tour guide takes about twenty people at a time to the sites on a bus. A tour of just one site takes a little over an hour, both takes three hours. Because only a small group can enter the passage at any one time, daily numbers are limited, so arrive early or go home with a long, disappointed face.

Birr Castle, County Offaly

40. Birr Castle

At one point during the nineteenth century, the name of Birr Castle could be heard on the lips of people all over the world. Yes, it was that famous. But more of that anon. Birr Castle still serves as a family home, although it's somewhat bigger than your average four-bedroom semi-detached, but that's rich feckers for ye.

The history bit

There's been a castle here in some form since 1170 but its been rebuilt, added to and expanded at various times, withstanding a few sieges in the process. Considering all of that, it's in an amazing state of preservation.

Take the lens cap off!!

The castle passed through various hands before the Parsons family took it over in 1620, and the present head of the family is the seventh Earl of Rosse, Brendan Parsons, who still lives here with his family. And it was thanks to one of his nineteenth-century ancestors that Birr earned world attention, particularly among scientists, when he built the world's largest telescope. Nicknamed the **'Leviathan'** of Parsonstown, the telescope held this record for over sixty years. It was a 183-cm reflecting scope and made international newspaper headlines, attracting hundreds of famous Victorian astronomy nerds to Birr. Among its many discoveries was the spiral structure of nebulae. The original Leviathan is on display in the castle grounds.

Past and future

That association with science explains the presence of the **Science Centre**, which features fancy interactive displays on the history of astronomy, photography and engineering, along with lots of the fascinating early instruments used in those pioneering experiments back in the old days.

The castle itself may only be visited by organised tours, which operate in the summer months. It *is* someone's home, after all. How would you like some eejit with a camera taking pics of you watching the telly in your living room? Within the beautiful grounds, however, you may roam free along the 8 km of gorgeous walking trails.

A couple of other bits while we're here. **The walled**

garden is reputed to have the **world's tallest hedge!** And one other tragic record. Mary Ward was one of the first female astronomers and highly respected in her time. She was also a cousin of the Parsons family. In 1869, William Parsons' sons had built a steam-powered car and they were giving Mary a ride when she fell off and under a wheel, and was killed instantly. It made her the **first recorded motor vehicle fatality** in the world. Other than that, everything about Birr Castle is an absolute joy!

Frankly we've only hired him to cut the hedges.

Round Tower, Clonmacnoise, County Offaly

41. Clonmacnoise

W e're a holy lot, us Irish, or at least we used to be. We'd never miss mass, regularly go to confession, we'd feel guilty about everything, especially lustful thoughts, and there was a picture of the Sacred Heart adorning

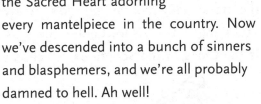

every mantelpiece in the country. Now we've descended into a bunch of sinners and blasphemers, and we're all probably damned to hell. Ah well!

The history bit

Anyway, one of the reasons for our Holy Joe culture can be traced all the way back to the powerful influence of early monks and priests, and the settlements they established. One of the most famous of all of these is Clonmacnoise, which was founded by St Ciarán in the sixth century. Thanks to the Shannon, which is just next to the site, access was easy for the faithful and for traders and artisans, so Clonmacnoise quickly developed into a large community. The ruins, most of which date from the tenth century or later, include a cathedral, seven churches, three High Crosses (one is incomplete) and two round towers, so no one was going to be short of an opportunity for a few words with the Man upstairs.

Holy stuff

There are lots of interesting bits and bobs to take in. The ancient graveyard, for example, has the largest collection of Early Christian grave slabs in Western Europe. In the tiny **Temple Ciarán**, excavations unearthed the **Clonmacnoise Crozier**, a gorgeous, highly decorated piece of Celtic artwork that's now in the National Museum. The three **High Crosses** on the site are actually replicas, but don't worry, you can see the real thing in the Visitor Centre, the most famed of which is the **Cross of the Scriptures**, which is a

The Clonmacnoise Crozier

Looks fantastic. Now, I want you to create an exact replica in case they put an interpretive centre here.

four-metre-high sandstone cross intricately carved with biblical scenes. A Celtic High Cross, by the way, is one with a ring around the centre of the cross, the ring representing the celestial sphere, whatever the hell that is.

The **Visitor Centre** is relatively small, but has the original three crosses, an audio-visual display explaining some of the history and an exhibition about the surrounding landscape. It's also a handy place to retreat to if it starts bucketing rain.

Lough Allen and the Arigna Mountains, County Roscommon

42. The Arigna Mining Experience

Time to don the hard hats, folks, we're heading below ground.

The Arigna Mines have been in operation in some form since the seventeenth century, although in the early days it was not coal they were after, but iron. When coal was discovered, the real mining began, and it continued right up to 1990, when the local power station closed and, with it, the mine's only customer. But miners are used to digging deep in a crisis, and a bunch of them have brought new life and new jobs to Arigna Mines by reinventing it as a tourist attraction, and a very interesting one at that.

The mine's location alone is reason enough to visit. It sits on the slopes of **Kilronan Hill** and has fine views of **Lough Allen** to the east. Inside the mine there's an exhibition of mining implements and equipment from Victorian days and you'll understand how a sardine feels after you see the conditions the miners worked in. It's sort of morbidly fascinating. Then you take the tour, which is done by an ex-miner and which takes you below the Arigna Hills. This is not for the claustrophobic. A soundtrack and lighting effects give you an authentic sense of what it was like, and the guides are usually good craic, spicing the facts with personal anecdotes.

After all that subterranean stuff, you might like to experience some overterranean scenery (we made up that word). Take a drive into the **Arigna Hills** that rise behind the mine entrance – there are some pleasant little roads to be explored that wander through woods, across bogs and through green valleys.

223

The grave of WB Yeats, Drumcliffe, County Sligo

43. Yeats Country

The peace comes dropping slow in County Sligo, to paraphrase the county's most famous son, William Butler Yeats, winner of the Nobel Prize for Literature and one of the most renowned poets in history. And you never know, you might be moved to poetry yourself when you experience some of Sligo's tremendous scenery, beaches, historic sights, villages and towns.

A man of his words

But let's start with Mr Yeats. He was actually a Dubliner, but spent much of his youth on his holliers in Sligo, which gave him a grá for the place. He moved here and came to regard it as his spiritual home. Yeats became fascinated by the county's landscape and its myths and legends, as, we believe, will you.

Among the most iconic mountains in Ireland, **Benbulben** (also spelled Benbulbin) inspired Yeats to pen 'Under Ben Bulben'. About 15 km north of Sligo town, it's a green-coated, plateau-topped ginormous chunk of limestone with great gullies cutting into its sides. A real 'wow' factor here. When you see the mountain, you'll understand.

But actually the hill most associated with Yeats is **Knocknarea**, which is just 5 km west of Sligo. And it's relatively easy to get to the top. There's a car park just to the south east of the hill, and a track to the top, which takes about twenty minutes to walk. At the top, the views of the coast and landscape are amazing. You'll also see the largest unexcavated and unopened passage tomb near the summit. Called **Queen Maeve's Cairn**, the huge structure is 55 metres wide and 10 metres high, and dates from about 3000 BC. Who knows what secrets it holds? But don't be tempted to try and find out!

Sligo Town is a pretty place on the **Garravogue River**. It's got a whole bunch of nice restaurants, hotels and pubs and a pleasant riverside walk. Among the things to watch out for are the **Yeats Memorial Building**, which is interesting, but frankly a bit banjaxed and shabby and in need of investment. It's not a fitting tribute to the great man.

Almost directly across the river is an unusual **bronze sculpture** of the poet. His body seems to balloon out of proportion to his head, the metal inscribed with lines of his poetry. And from a certain angle it looks like Yeats is giving us the finger. Maybe he is. Or maybe he's telling us what he thinks of the Memorial Building.

About 8 km north of Sligo you'll come to **Drumcliff**, just off the main road. There's a church and a small cemetery beside it, which is Yeats's final resting place and probably the most visited grave in Ireland. It famously bears the epitaph that Yeats penned himself: 'Cast a cold Eye/On Life, on Death/ Horseman, pass by.'

Just past Drumcliff take the L3305 on the left, which after 7 km will take you to **Lissadell House**, a splendid, neo-classical country house you can tour and with a fab **Alpine garden** overlooking the Atlantic. There are also woodland walks and a beach. The house has close associations with Yeats and Constance Markievicz. Who the hell is that, you ask? Well, she was one of the leaders of the 1916 Rising (very unusual to have a woman military leader back then), and she was the first woman elected to the British Parliament, though she never took her seat. She was also a suffragette, a charity worker and a socialist activist, so she kept a lot of balls in the air!

But let's leave Yeats to sum up Sligo in a handful of words:

'There are no strangers here; only friends you haven't met.'

The Rock of Cashel, County Tipperary

44. The Rock of Cashel

Take a walled medieval fortress, a Gothic cathedral, a Romanesque chapel, a towering bishop's residence, an ecclesiastical hall, an ancient round tower and cram them onto an area of about 200 square metres on a high rocky outcrop overlooking grassy plains, and you've got the awesome Rock of Cashel. You've probably seen it before, you know, in the background in any number of swords and princesses movies from the 1950s and 1960s. It also featured in the Stanley Kubrick classic movie *Barry Lyndon* and John

Boorman's *Excalibur*. It's currently up for UNESCO World Heritage status, which is actually long overdue. (C'mon, UNESCO guys, get your act together!) The best place to take a pic of the Rock is a bit north along either the R660 or the R639.

The history bit

Back in the ninth century, the Rock was the seat of the kings of Munster. One of Ireland's most famed kings, Brian Boru, was crowned King of Munster here in 978. But then in 1101, it turned all religiousy when Brian's great grandson and King of Munster, Muirchertach Ua Briain, (try pronouncing that when you've had a few pints), decided to present the location to the church.

Murky tash ooh breen (hic).

It then developed into a major religious centre, famed for its medieval architecture and collection of Celtic art. **The Round Tower** was completed around 1100 and **Cormac's Chapel** in 1134. In 1152, with the approval of Rome, Ireland was to set up four archbishoprics, at Dublin, Armagh, Tuam and, of course, Cashel. From then on, the Archbishop of Cashel resided there, and, of course, no archbishop could be without his own fancy **Cathedral**, which was completed in 1270, followed by a nice, comfy gaff with the **Archbishop's Residence**. **The Hall of the**

Vicars Choral was added about two centuries later.

In 1647, Ireland was in the midst of the Confederate Wars, which cost about a quarter of a million Irish lives, and mostly involved Oliver Cromwell's forces butchering every Irish man, woman, and child who looked crooked at him. One of his Irish allies, Murrough MacDermod O'Brien, sacked the Rock, massacred everyone and then looted and destroyed a great deal of the site's treasures. Cashel was pretty much destroyed as a place of religious worship, until the twentieth century, when it became a place of tourist worship. Queen Elizabeth II specifically asked to visit Cashel on her historic visit to Ireland in 2011, probably to see if there was anything left that her ancestors hadn't nicked.

The bits to see

The Round Tower is in the classic design of this particularly Irish monastic icon. Some of Ireland's myriad round towers date from before the ninth century when they were used as bell towers and a place of refuge, usually from raiding Vikings. This one is almost 30 metres high and its entrance is almost four metres off the ground.

Cormac's Chapel is a small but magnificent Romanesque

church that was consecrated in 1134. It is a sophisticated structure, with vaulted ceilings and wide arches, a carved tympanum (a semi-circular decorative yoke over an entrance, door or window) over both doorways, and it contains one of the best-preserved Irish frescoes from the medieval period.

The Cathedral was finished in 1270, which must have been a relief to the workers as the feckin' thing took nearly forty years to put up. Unfortunately the roof is gone, thanks to Anglican archbishop Arthur Price, who decided to remove it, for reasons known only to his own idiotic self, in 1749. But there's still much to admire. The most attractive elements are the transepts (c.1270), with triple lancet windows. On the east side of the transepts (the arm bits of the cross-shape) are square chapels, all with piscinae (stone basins) and three with tomb niches. The north transept contains late medieval tombs. At the western end of the nave is the five-storey bishop's residence – presumably he needed all the floors to get nearer to God.

You actually enter the site via the **Hall of the Vicars Choral**, built in the fifteenth century. The Hall was restored in connection with the European Architectural Heritage Year (1975). It housed the minor clerics appointed to sing and chant during cathedral services. The furniture is original, the vaulted timber roof was reconstructed to medieval specifications. The large wall tapestry, showing King Solomon with the Queen of Sheba, contains intentional errors to remind viewers that only God can create perfection, or at least that's the excuse the artist used when he finished and realised he'd made a hames of it.

Beyond the buildings lie the walled grounds, home to long-dead priests, monks and posh dudes. Some of the graves are really, really old and lots are marked with Irish High Crosses.

Cashel Town

Luckily you're never far from a pint or a steak or whatever you fancy when you visit the Rock, as it's only 500 metres from the centre of the pretty town of Cashel, which has some very good traditional Irish pubs and a fine selection of restaurants. There's also a lot of history to explore in Cashel and its immediate surroundings.

Cashel Folk Village is an old-world museum containing a fab collection of historical memorabilia related to Ireland's War of Independence, when we finally kicked the Brits out! (If you're British, you and your wallet are very welcome back now!) There is also a section of the museum documenting The Great Irish Famine of 1845–1851. In the 1916 Easter Rising section you get a great sense of that period of Irish history, thanks to the vast array of original memorabilia on display.

The Bolton Library contains the finest collection of antiquarian books outside of Dublin, including the twelfth-century Nuremberg Chronicle, and works by Dante, Swift,

Calvin, Erasmus and Machiavelli.

The **Heritage Centre** is on Cashel's main street. A large-scale model of the town in the 1640s highlights the area's lesser-known treasures. Multi-lingual audio commentary is available. You can also see the Charters of Cashel by Charles II (in 1663) and James II (in 1687), on permanent display. And to cap it all, admission is free. Yippee!

Hore Abbey is actually visible from the Rock of Cashel walls. Don't worry, it's not named so because the monks were addicted to medieval hookers, but because 'hore' derives from the Irish word 'iubhair', meaning yew tree. The ruins are quite impressive, and date from the late thirteenth century.

I didn't know it was spelt H-O-R-E when I signed up to become a monk.

Kilmacthomas Viaduct, Waterford Greenway

45. Waterford and the Greenway

We have the Vikings largely to thank for the existence of Waterford City, as they came a-plundering here in the ninth century. They eventually built the city around 914, making it Ireland's oldest, then started hitting it off with the local cailíns and there were soon lots of little half-Irish half-Viking kiddies running about.

On the other hand, maybe there's no rush getting back to Scandinavia ...

Stuff to visit

The Viking heritage is still much in evidence in the fine city. **Reginald's Tower** was built on the site of a Viking stronghold and takes its name from a Viking ruler called Ragnall. The medieval building has a Viking exhibition including artefacts, models and the weapons they used to chop off bits of people. Outside is a replica of a **Viking longboat**.

The **Medieval Museum** is in a very trendy building that incorporates the really modern with the really ancient. It also has some Viking stuff, but it spans a much broader era. It has loads of interesting artefacts such as the city's amazing, illustrated four-metre-long charter roll from 1373, and King Henry VIII's hat! There's also a fifteenth-century wine cellar and a thirteenth-century Choristers' Hall.

The Bishop's Palace is Waterford's other well-known museum, dedicated to the city's later history. The eighteenth-century building's a gem inside and out, and is filled with historical gems, like the oldest piece of Waterford Crystal in the world, and a lock of Napoleon's hair. Its elegant rooms are filled with original furniture, paintings and silverware.

If you're driving, you might like to explore a little, and about thirty minutes' drive west you'll find the **Comeragh Mountains**. There's a sign-posted scenic route to be explored, and among the most popular attractions is **Mahon Falls**. Another fab scenic drive is along the **Copper Coast**, from Tramore to Dungarvan, so called after the copper mines that used to operate here. The scenery is simply splendiferously sumptuous.

If you're not driving, another increasingly popular way to explore is the recently opened **Waterford Greenway**, a dedicated cycling/walking route that runs from Waterford City to Dungarvan along 46 km of converted railway line. It crosses three towering viaducts, goes through a 400-metre tunnel and passes loads of historic Viking or medieval

ruins, a famine workhouse and old railway stations. And you'll probably be so thirsty when you reach Dungarvan, you'll drink the place dry.

But you couldn't have picked a nicer spot to do just that! **Dungarvan** is a lovely spot built around a harbour and a nice town square. There's a pleasant waterfront area with a choice of eateries and drinkeries, and the town in general is well served in that regard. There are also plenty of interesting historic bits to see, and lots of walks in which to indulge your legs and lungs.

Dunbrody Famine Ship, New Ross, County Wexford

46. Dunbrody Famine Ship

If you're Canadian or American with some Irish blood (and who doesn't have some?) you may owe your very existence to the original Dunbrody ship. The Dunbrody Famine Ship is an exact replica of that which transported gazillions of Irish men and women to Quebec who were trying to escape the ravages of the Great Famine. You never know, perhaps one of those emigrants was your great-great-great-great granny or grandad.

The ship is a real one that has participated in the Tall Ships Festival and sailed as far as Wales, but it's been docked in New Ross now since 2006 and it's not going anywhere soon, given its popularity.

Anchors aweigh!

There's a small but interesting museum before you board, with exhibits of the ticket office and the peasants awaiting departure – the cheapest ticket, incidentally, cost three pounds, or three months' pay! You then board the ship for a guided tour, which is performed by actors in costume playing the roles of famine-era emigrants. It's an entertaining way to learn about the sewer-smelling, disease-ridden, rat-infested conditions in which the emigrants travelled! With the help of the guides and your own imagination, you can get a sense of the nightmarish and claustrophobic journey it must have been.

After you emerge from the ship's bowels, you then move back onto terra firma and the **Irish America Hall of Fame**, which is a fascinating look at the contribution Irish emigrants made to American history. Here's a thought – JFK's granddaddy was from Wexford and probably departed here on a ship just like the Dunbrody. The thing is that his assassin, Lee Harvey Oswald's great grandmother was also an Irish emigrant. You win some, you lose some!

The stench, crowds and diseases are all-inclusive.

RAT TRAVEL INC.

On the subject of JFK, you might also like to visit the **Kennedy Homestead**, about 5 km south of New Ross, and then a few kilometres further south, lies the gorgeous 600-acre **Kennedy Arboretum**. Yep, there's a lot of Kennedy stuff in Wexford!

The Upper Lake, Glendalough, County Wicklow

47. Glendalough

If scenery, history, woodlands, archaeology, nature, walking or relaxing are your thing, Glendalough is the place for you. And all of it is within relatively easy reach of Dublin. The only feckin' problem is that, especially at weekends, you may have to fend off hordes of fellow tourists in order to get your snaps. But don't let that deter you, as once you escape to the upper lough and the surrounding hills and walking trails, peace and calm will wrap you in a warm blanket.

Glendalough, or Gleann Dá Loch in its original form, means 'valley of the two loughs'. It was formed by a glacier during the last ice age, so it's really only a mere snapper geologically speaking. But that glacier left behind behind an area that has entranced and inspired people for thousands of years.

The history bit

Sometime in the sixth century, a local lad called Kevin was believed by his parents to have divine powers, or some ould shite, so they packed him off to become a monk, which was the medieval equivalent of getting rid of the kids by sending them to summer camp. Years later, Kevin discovered Glendalough and decided it was so tranquil and beautiful that it would be the ideal place to commune with God.

Kevin lived as a hermit and spent a lot of his time in a cramped man-made cave now known as **St Kevin's Bed** and the rest of his time talking to the local wildlife and occasionally beating it to death for his dinner. His dedication was such that it inspired loads of other monks to move to Glendalough, and a community sprang up. It flourished for six centuries and became an important place of pilgrimage.

Unfortunately it also became an important place for the raping and pillaging Vikings. In fact, oak taken from

Glendalough was used to build the second-largest Viking longboat every recorded and a good part of that ship still exists, although you'll have to go to Denmark to see it.

In 1128, St Laurence O'Toole, probably the second most revered Irish saint after St Paddy himself, became Abbot of Glendalough and unlike the parsimonious St Kevin, he was famous for his hospitality and liked to throw big shindigs. But he also used to atone for his sins by taking up residence in St Kevin's bed during Lent.

By the time Glendalough's influence began to wane, there was a whole caboodle of monastic buildings, and the ruins of many of these may still be seen, including the iconic Round Tower (see below).

The main monastic bits

The Gateway to the monastic village is unique in Ireland in that it was originally two-storeyed. Sadly the upper storey has long vanished, its stones probably nicked by some local to build a pub. The paving within is the original, so you are literally walking in the footsteps of the medieval monks.

The aforementioned **Round Tower** is one of Ireland's most recognisable images. There are lots of similar round towers still standing around the country, but few with such an impressive setting. It's 30 metres high, built of schist and granite, in case you really wanted to know, and it was built as a bell tower and as a place to hide from smelly Vikings. This last explains why the entrance is nearly four metres off the ground. The four windows on the top level face north, south, east and west.

The **Cathedral** is the largest of the ruins at the monastic site. By later cathedral standards, it's pretty small, but a thousand years ago it was considered ginormous. The main part was built around 950, with other bits added over the next few centuries. The roof is gone, sadly, but the nave is pretty much intact, and part of the decorated central arch still remains.

A stone's throw to the south of the Cathedral is one of the best-preserved buildings, **St Kevin's Church**. Its skilfully constructed roof is made from overlapping stones and it has a mini-round tower. The powers-that-be have decided that us lowly types shouldn't be allowed inside, so you can only peek into the shadows though a gate.

There's a whole pile of other ruins speckled about the place, including **Trinity Church**, **St Mary's Church**, **The**

Priests' House, **St Ciarán's Church** and **St Saviour's Church**. There are even more ruins around the Upper Lough, including **Reefert Church**, which nestles in a grove of trees, its meaning 'the place of the kings'. There is also a small church called **Teampall na Skellig** on the southern side of the Upper Lough that can only be reached by boat. It may be seen from the other side of the lough with binoculars or really sharp eyesight. Just 40 metres east is **St Kevin's Bed**, which is a cramped, man-made hollow cut into the cliff-face, where the old saint used to curl up with a good bible before sleeping on the jagged rocks. Comfy.

The Visitor Centre

There is a modern Visitor Centre located just to the east of the monastic site with lots of interesting exhibits and an audio-visual show. There is also a model of what the whole site looked like, complete with the long-gone peasant huts, walls and farming enclosures. Guided tours of the monastic site may be arranged through the centre.

Walking trails and wildlife

There is a whole bunch of tracks around the lakes, suitable for everyone, from the laziest doss artist on the planet to the fitness fanatic. There are nine different, colour-coded, way-marked routes ranging from a short stroll up to a four-hour hike. Among the creatures you might well encounter are feral goats, badgers, red Sika deer, red squirrels, rabbits and stoats. Otters are frequently seen in the lakes and streams. The woodlands boast lots of bird species, such as the wren, chaffinch, blackbird, jay, sparrowhawk, wood warbler and redstart. Herons and cormorants feed in the river and lakes, which are rich in brown trout. You can buy a handy little leaflet in the Visitor Centre, which details all the walking routes.

Put your feet up

After all that walking, you'll need a pint or six, and the area has numerous options for eating and drinking. In Glendalough itself there's a hotel, which has a restaurant and a pub that serves food. Just over a kilometre away to the east is the small village of Laragh, which offers another small hotel and a selection of nice pubs where you can relax, stuff your gob and get langered in luxurious surroundings as you reflect on poor St Kevin starving himself in a cave with pointy rocks sticking into his arse.

245

Avondale House, County Wicklow

48. Avondale House and Forest Park

Charles Stewart Parnell was one of the greatest political leaders in Irish history, and Avondale is his birthplace and home. He certainly had plenty of space to play hide and seek in when he was a nipper, as the surrounding estate is over 500 acres.

The history bit

Parnell's greatest achievement was in the area of land rights. You see, the Brits had come in and stolen all our land over the centuries and Parnell basically forced them to hand it back, bit by bit, using a campaign of peaceful non-co-operation and boycotting. (There's a fantastic novel about all that called *Boycott*. Can't think of the author's name!) He also brought Ireland to the brink of Home Rule, before he was undone by a scandalous love afair with another MP's missus. Tut tut. You'll probably learn a lot about this on a tour of the house.

Have you read this book about Boycott?

No, I'm boycotting it.

Home sweet home

Avondale is not a palatial country mansion, but it is a large and attractive house that dates from 1777. You get to explore the various beautiful rooms, including Parnell's office and bedroom, which contain either original or replica period furniture. Remember to look up and admire the stucco (that's plasterwork to the ordinary Joe Soap), which was created by the world-renowned Lafranchini brothers. After your tour, you might like to grab a bite to eat in the basement café.

Out and about

Fed and watered, it's time to get out and explore. The Parnell family were landlords and there is a certain irony in the fact that someone who owned so much land was a champion of the downtrodden peasant farmer, waging a peaceful war against his fellow landlords. Nowadays much of the land is given over to trees and walks, and there are plenty of both. There are many different trails you can explore through the glorious woodlands, which are populated with a huge variety of species. Best seen in the autumn, of course, but its frankly gorgeous any time. If the weather's nice (and good luck with that), it's a perfect place for a picnic.

Avondale is history and nature all in the same spot. What more could you ask for?

Powerscourt House, County Wicklow

49. Powerscourt House and Gardens

That title's a teensy-weensy bit misleading, as while there is a magnificent mansion here, you can only visit a little bit of it. But really you're here for the estate and garden, which is one of the most magnificent on the planet – no kidding.

The history bit

The house was originally a fourteenth-century castle but was developed into a large mansion in the mid-eighteenth century by the Powerscourt clan, who were all lord and lady-types with money to burn. They also had the gardens developed – a job that took twenty years to complete. And you moan about the twenty minutes it takes to mow the lawn. In 1961, that family finally relinquished their treasured

250

home and sold it to the Slazenger brood – yes, they're folk who make tennis racquets and golf balls and so on. Tragically, in 1974, a fire almost completely destroyed the building. It stood as a blackened shell until it was completely restored in 1997. Nowadays part of the house serves as a retail outlet. Yes, that sounds wojus but the stores are all of the Irish craft/artisan/'Jaysus that's expensive' variety, and therefore quite tasteful.

Garden heaven

But by far the highlight of any visit to Powerscourt is the **gardens**, which *National Geographic* named as the third most beautiful on the planet. From the house they sweep majestically down to tiled or grassy terraces and a gorgeous fountained pond beyond. Topiary and flowerbeds exploding with colour abound, and beyond the lawns, woodlands give way to a view of the quartz-peaked Great Sugar Loaf mountain. The view would leave you lost for eh...em...uh.

Besides the main view from the house, the estate also boasts **The Walled Gardens**, **The Italian Garden**, **The Dolphin Pond**, **The Japanese Gardens**, **Pets Cemetery** and **Pepperpot Tower**. And a short drive away you can see **Powerscourt Waterfall**, which is Ireland's highest. OK, Victoria Falls it ain't, but it's a favourite spot for picnickers and people who like waterfalls.

THE DOLPHIN POND

251

Wicklow Gaol, Wicklow Town

50. Wicklow Gaol

Fancy a bit of ghost hunting? Wicklow Gaol claims to be one of the world's most haunted buildings and has featured in an episode of the TV show *Ghost Hunters International*. But as regards their claims about ghosts, well, you can see right through them...

The history bit

Besides the paranormal stuff, the gaol has a fascinating tale to tell and one that encompasses a broad sweep of modern Irish history. Its inmates included rebels captured during the 1798 rebellion, who were probably lucky as most of the captured volunteers were brutally slaughtered along with thousands of civilians. But hey, who's holding grudges? (Mutters 'murdering scumbags' to self.) During the Great Famine, the gaol became overwhelmed with prisoners, many of whom had deliberately committed a crime to be imprisoned, where at least they'd be fed. It was also used to house prisoners during the Irish War of Independence and the Civil War in the 1920s. What better way to spend a couple of hours than recalling two centuries of misery, torture, brutality and starvation!

That's the spirit

Seriously, it's a great tour of the historic building with state-of-the-art audio-visual doo-dahs, mannequin guards and prisoners and sound effects. Actors in costume conduct you to cells and dungeons and onto a replica of a ship that transported prisoners to Van Diemen's Land (today known as Tasmania). It's certainly a creepy place and although it closed its doors as a prison in 1924, some prisoners are reputedly still hanging around the place, maybe even from a rope... On certain dates, you can actually do the tour at night and there's even a special 'Paranormal Tour'. Around Halloween, these tours are jammers with people dressed as zombies, vampires, skeletons etc. It's great craic altogether!

And talking of Halloween. Has it ever occurred to you that Halloween parties in nudist colonies must be really boring?

You can't beat Wicklow Gaol for a really good incarceration.

A Feckin' Tour of Ireland: Essential Irish Slang

Banjaxed (adj): Damaged beyond repair/very tired

Blather (n): Bullshit

Bowsie (n): Disreputable character, good-for-nothing

Brutal (adj): Awful, hideous

Craic (n) (pronounced 'crack'): Fun, chatter, laughter, drinking

Cute hoor (n): Resourceful person of dubious character

Deadly (adj): Great, brilliant

Dosh (n): Money

Dosser (n): A good-for-nothing person

Eejit (n): Naïve or stupid person

Fair play to you (expr): Well done! Good man!

Fecker (n): Person

Feckin' (adj): PC version of 'f' word'

Gaff (n): House or place

Ganky (adj): Disgusting, repulsive

Gansey-load (expr): A great many

Gawk (n) (v): A look/to look at

Gazillion (n): A very large number

Geebag (n): Unpleasant woman

Gee-eyed (adj): Really, really drunk

Ginormous (adj): Really, really big

Gobshite (n): Stupid, horrible person

Gouger (n): Sly, repulsive person

In the nip (expr): Nude

Jacks (n): The toilet/bathroom

Jammy (adj): Lucky

Kip (n): Horrible place

Make a hames of (expr): Make a complete mess of

Manky (adj): Really dirty

Mortified (adj): Very embarrassed

Mot (n): Girl, girlfriend

On the lash (expr): On a drinking session

Rat-arsed (adj): Really, really, drunk

Shite (n): Crap, faeces; (adj) Poor quality

Spondulicks (n): Bank notes/money

Wagon (n): Horrible or nasty woman

Wojus (adj): Utterly useless

Yoke (n): Any object, a thing

Yonks (n): A very long time

 **Colin Murphy** is the co-author of nineteen Feckin' books as well numerous other humorous books on Irish life and culture. He has also written an acclaimed Irish historical novel, *Boycott*, and three non-fiction history books. When he's not writin' feckin' books, he spends his time wandering Ireland's mountains. He is married to Gráinne, and they have two adult kids, Emmet and Ciára.

 **Brendan O'Reilly** is an illustrator and senior art director in the world of advertising, and a book cover designer. He likes to relax by moaning and complaining about the state of the country over a pint or five, and he also likes to tramp up and down the hills and explore the wilderness. He is married to Bernie, and they have two children, Vincent and Isobel.